SO-FKR-866

Daniel Manin, and Venice in 1848-49, Tr. by
Charles Martel, With an Intr. by I. Butt

You are holding a reproduction of an original work that is in the public domain in the United States of America, and possibly other countries.You may freely copy and distribute this work as no entity (individual or corporate) has a copyright on the body of the work.This book may contain prior copyright references, and library stamps (as most of these works were scanned from library copies).These have been scanned and retained as part of the historical artifact.

This book may have occasional imperfections such as missing or blurred pages, poor pictures, errant marks, etc. that were either part of the original artifact, or were introduced by the scanning process. We believe this work is culturally important, and despite the imperfections, have elected to bring it back into print as part of our continuing commitment to the preservation of printed works worldwide. We appreciate your understanding of the imperfections in the preservation process, and hope you enjoy this valuable book.

DANIEL MANIN,

AND

VENICE IN 1848-49.

BY
HENRI MARTIN,
AUTHOR OF "L'HISTOIRE DE FRANCE."
(TRANSLATED BY CHARLES MARTEL.)

WITH AN INTRODUCTION
BY ISAAC BUTT, Q.C., M.P.
AUTHOR OF "THE HISTORY OF ITALY."

IN TWO VOLUMES.
VOL. I.

LONDON:
CHARLES J. SKEET, PUBLISHER,
10, KING WILLIAM STREET,
CHARING CROSS.
1862.

200. k. 74.

246. b. 165.

BILLING, PRINTER AND STEREOTYPER, GUILDFORD, SURREY.

CONTENTS OF VOL. I.

CHAPTER III.

CHAPTER IV.

CHAPTER V.

.INTRODUCTION.

(BY ISAAC BUTT, ESQ., M.P.)

I HAVE been requested to supply a few pages of introduction to an English translation of Henri Martin's history of Daniel Manin in connection with the Venetian Revolution of 1848. The French work was published in Paris in the year 1859. That year naturally produced from the press of France many publications illustrating the incidents and episodes of modern Italian history; among these incidents the struggle of Venice occupied a conspicuous place, and among the publications which made the French people acquainted with the details of that struggle, "Daniel Manin, par Henri Martin," enjoyed a fame and a popularity worthy of the genius and the reputation of its author. If the translator has worthily executed his task, these volumes present to the reader the story of a noble struggle fittingly told.

That story in its main features is a short one. On the 22nd of March, 1848, the population of Venice expelled the Austrian garrison, and Venice was again free. On the 22nd of August, 1849, the beleaguered city was compelled to yield to the overwhelming force that invested her, and the Austrian power was once more throughout Italy supreme.

Throughout this short but glorious struggle, the Venetian people displayed those qualities of moderation and self-command which have in the last two years attracted to the Italian cause the astonished admiration of Europe, while the latter months of that struggle were made memorable by a resistance as heroic as any which the annals of history record.

The patriot and the hero of this struggle was Daniel Manin. An advocate pursuing his profession in the limited sphere which the despotic jurisprudence of Austria permitted, he became the inmate of a prison for his attachment to liberal opinions. Brought from that prison to guide the movements of his countrymen, he was entrusted by them with the powers of their dictator. His name is inseparably associated with "Venice in 1848 and 1849." He it was who guided and controlled the revolution. The leader in the cause of his country's freedom, he was its martyr. It was not his fortune to die for Venice either on the scaffold or in the field, but a slower, a far more torturing martyrdom awaited him during the eight years which he passed in exile and want—witnessing the sorrows and sufferings of those dearest to him, until at last he found repose himself in a foreign grave far from the country which he loved.

Estimated by the impression he has left among his countrymen, he must have been an extraordinary man. No name is held in equal veneration, no memory so fondly cherished throughout Northern Italy as that of Daniel Manin. Eight years after he had left Venice in disaster and defeat, his death was mourned by the whole population as a national calamity. Every Italian is ready to acknowledge the justice of the title which French writers have conferred on him, that of "the great exile of Venice," or even of the higher one which has been given to him by

the critics of our own less excitable country,
"the noblest and wisest of Italian patriots."*

The history of this struggle possesses at least
one strange interest. It is the solitary instance
in which Venice ever rose in arms against her
oppressors.

It is impossible for the mind susceptible of
the influence of historic associations to contemplate without emotion anything connected with
the fortunes of Venice. When treachery and
fraud destroyed her independence in 1797,
that independence had existed undisturbed for
more than 1300 years. Through that long lapse
of centuries no invader had ever succeeded in
planting the tyranny of foreign rule in her island
home. The soil on which the city was built
was scarcely reclaimed from the waves of the
sea ; a shallow expanse of water alone separated
her from the land, which was lorded over by
great and ambitious potentates. Her whole
territory could not grow food to sustain one-tenth
of her population. Yet, through every vicissi-
tude of Europe and of Italy, Venice had been
free. She had seen the Western empire of the

* Edinburgh Review.

Romans fall, and the Byzantine Cæsars yield
to the Moslem—she had witnessed in her long
existence the incursions of the Lombards, the
fall of their dynasty before the conquering arms
of the great Charles, and the establishment of
the new empire of the West. Her memories
and her records extended back before the origin
of the Papal power. Venice was a nation when
Otho asserted for the elective Kings of Germany the succession to the imperial crown of
Charlemagne. She had witnessed the rise and
the downfall of the great Republics which once
gave glory and freedom to Italy. In her tran-
quil neutrality she had been a spectator of the
struggles of the cities of the Lombard league ;
she had mediated the peace which finally secured
the liberties of the cities, and beneath the dome of
St. Mark. had taken place that memorable interview between Barbarossa and the patriot
pontiff, which reconciled Imperial power to
Italy and to the Church. She had witnessed
the enslavement of all the cities of the league,
and her republican government in its haughty
independence survived the subjugation of the
country under Charles V. Through all the

changes and chances of those varied scenes—
throughout the whole long struggles of Europe
in the centuries which connect the days of the
Roman empire with those of the French revolution, the stranger had never once desecrated with a
conquering army the island that rose near "the
deep river," the "Rialto," where Venetian freedom had found its shelter and made its home.

Venice stands alone in the history of the world.
In her origin, her greatness, her domestic policy,
even in the site and architecture of her buildings,
she was like no city that had ever been on earth.
Early in the fifth century, the incursions of the
barbarians drove some of the inhabitants of
Northern Italy, the Veneti of ancient history,
to take shelter in a wild waste of sand and
water which bordered the coast, where the
great rivers that crossed the Lombard plains
poured themselves in sluggish and diffuse
channels into the Adriatic. The desolate swamps
of Carolina could not have presented a less
promising habitation. Upon one of the banks
which rose a little above the watery surface of
the lagoon a few sheds served the purpose of
temporary stores, to receive the cargoes of the

galleys that made their way with difficulty
through the intricacies of the channel; upon
some others, a few gardens and bathing lodges
had been formed. But over the greater extent
of this singular conformation these banks were
used only for the purpose of salt pans, or
on their barren sands fishermen disputed with
the vast flocks of sea-fowl a place to spread
their nets. In the islands of these lagoons
successive companies of fugitives found shelter
and erected habitations, protected from pursuit
by the nature of the terraqueous channel
which separated them from the terra firma.
Too shallow for vessels, yet here and there
intersected by treacherous gullies that were
too deep to be forded, this salt lake interposed an impassable barrier to all who were
not thoroughly acquainted with its passes. Towards the sea-side, it would seem the inhabitants endeavoured to guard themselves from
the incursions of the waves by rude defences of
wicker-work, against which, in time, the sand
and the alluvial deposits accumulated. Scattered
over these banks, the fugitives lived " like sea
birds," obtaining almost their whole subsistence

from the occupations of fishing and making salt. Such was the origin of the Venetian nation.

From that time to this the history of that nation has been one long romance. Near the deepest of the channels that intersected these lagoons the city of Venice gradually rose and became the capital of the communes that were scattered far over the islands along the coast.*

* A decree of the senate of Pavia is still preserved, bearing date in 421, desiring the fugitives scattered over the islands of the Lagune to unite on that of the Rialto, for the purpose of forming a city and building a fleet. But Torcello and other islands were subsequently fixed on as the successive capitals of the confederation. Malacomo was so when Pepin invaded the Lagune. His invasion caused the transfer of the seat of government to the less accessible island of the Rialto, and from this date the foundation of the modern city of Venice may properly be reckoned.

Although successful in storming Malacomo, the armies of Pepin, in attempting to pursue the inhabitants across the shallows of the Lagune, sustained a complete and signal defeat.

The island of the Rialto derives its name, according to some, from "rivum altum," the deep channel which flows past it—the name, indeed, of a river which is traced from the Alps to that portion of the Lagune; others derive it from "ripa alta," the high bank.

The city seemed to rise literally from the sea; her foundations were in the waters, and her buildings were washed by the waves. A channel of the sea supplied the place of a street, and her inhabitants traversed the city in boats. Before long, commerce began to enrich the infant state. In the progress of time the traffic of the East poured its wealth into her lap. Her merchant princes vied with the sovereigns of the world. A great maritime population supplied her with elements of strength; a numerous navy and a well-replenished exchequer made her a formidable power. Distant colonies extended her dominion on the farthest shores that were washed by the waters of the Mediterranean. Her navies visited every portion of that sea, then the centre of the civilization and commerce of the world. The ambassadors of the greatest potentates came humbly to her citizen princes in her audience halls; and the successors of the fugitive fishermen and salt gatherers dictated their commands to distant countries from palaces that had risen upon the very spot where their ancestors scarcely found room to spread their nets, or erect the rude sheds which barely gave them shelter from the elements of heaven.

The constitution of Venice shared in the singularity which belonged to everything con-nected with the state. The first settlers in the lagoon were not long in discovering the neces-sity of combining for mutual defence. It was not, however, until after two centuries had been spent in imperfect attempts at this combination that they united themselves under one chief of the republic. In the year 697 Anafesto was elected the first doge or duke; and the form of government then established lasted substantially until 1100 years afterwards the last doge of Venice, the successor of Anafesto, was deposed.

Little understood by foreign nations, the go-vernment of Venice possessed attributes calcu-lated to impress strangers with a mysterious awe. Its far-famed and terrible council of ten —the secrecy that invested its political tribunals —still more that which surrounded the execution of their sentences—the stern majesty which was thrown round her magistrates bound them-selves by laws which the highest dare not violate with impunity—the gloomy state prisons from which many a captive was be-lieved never to come forth—the terror which was

inspired by many a punishment which fell
without warning and from unknown hands upon
the noblest in the republic—still darker stories
in which fear exaggerated the reality—all con-
spired to surround the Venetian constitution with
an air of gloomy grandeur that impressed the
imagination with a mixed feeling of terror and
respect.

There were two elements in the life of Venice
which exercised a powerful influence on the character of her people—their maritime occupations
and their intercourse with the East. It was the
policy of the Venetian republic to isolate herself
from the rest of Italy. The very position of
the city detached the people from the land.
Hence it was that these elements impressed
upon Venice a more distinguishing characteristic than they did upon the other great maritime cities. A nation of merchants and sailors
insensibly acquires traits of character drawn from
the influence of foreign lands. The attentive
observer will easily discern in the institutions
and the character of the Venetians a subdued
orientalism which we have no difficulty in re-
ferring to their constant commerce with the

East. Possibly to the same source we may trace
the mystery and the secrecy which attended the
punishments inflicted upon traitors. Stories were
told of those who crossed the Bridge of Sighs,
and were never known to emerge from the prison
which that bridge connects with the palace of
the Doge. Of their fate nothing more was
heard than might be gathered from the story
of some gondolier who saw a burden borne at
midnight from the prison,—followed by a splash
in the canal. Tales like these, still more those
of malefactors plunged from a trap door into
unknown depths of water, without any one
asking after their mysterious fate — suggest
at once the incidents of Constantinople and
eastern vengeance.

The influence of the same associations may
be traced in the terrible announcement which
was sometimes made of the traitor's doom. A
lifeless corpse found suspended in the Piazzetta
in the morning, has given to Venice the first
intimation that treason has been discovered
within her walls, and that one of her noblest
citizens has been executed for the crime. In
the evening he was free and honoured; in the

morning his body told his astonished fellow-
citizens of his fate. Of his crime, his trial, or
his execution nothing more was known than the
meagre record of the scroll on the column from
which he was suspended, and its legend—
" Thus does Venice deal with traitors against
the state."

To the combined effects of oriental impressions
and those derived from occupation in the deep
waters is due, perhaps, the susceptibility of the
Venetians not only to religious feeling, but to a
belief in the marvellous which is often allied
with it. No city on earth has so many legends
of saints and miracles; in none were they so
implicitly and reverentially believed. But even
about the wildest of them there was a poetry
and a grandeur that elevated them far above
the grovelling superstitions by which in other
places religion was debased. How much of this
may be owing to the spirit of poetry which was
certainly brought from those eastern climes
from which their legends tell us their merchants
bore the precious relics of St. Mark? The
tendency of sailors to believe in the supernatural
has been in all ages remarked. The observation

is as old as the days of David of the influence of
"going down to the sea in ships, of doing business in great waters," in disposing men to faith
in the unseen.   And if the visitor at Venice is
even now struck by the many votive churches
which attest the reality in her earlier times of
a deep and reverential faith; if he is sur-
prised to find belief still strong in the traditions
of the marvellous narratives of bygone ages, he
may, perhaps, think it not unreasonable to attri-
bute this remarkable trait of the Venetian mind
to impressions received from traversing those
wild wastes of waters over which few have
ever passed without a conviction of the supernatural—or to beliefs brought home from those
eastern climes which were the cradle of the
human race—lands which the memories and
the susceptibilities of man's infancy still haunt.

The site and the architecture of Venice har-
monized strangely with the unique character of
her history and her institutions.   The poet came
nearest to the impression produced by the city
of the sea, who said, that other cities were built
by men, but Venice was the creation of gods.

In the strange sight of her long rows of palaces

rising from the waves, in the noiseless rush of the gondola through her watery streets, there is something altogether different from every-thing else in the cities of the world. Even in the style of the architecture we can discern the traits of her national character. The oriental arabesque is scarcely softened down to the less gorgeous beauty of the Italian style, while in the Gothic arches that . are seen in many, especially of her public buildings, we may with-out fancy trace the representative of another and distinct element in her national cha-racter.

The ancient glories of Venice are gone, but not long enough to obliterate their memory from the minds of a people before whose eyes their mo-numents and their memorials still stand un-touched. Sixty-four years have passed away since the Queen of the Adriatic yielded to the domi-nion of the stranger. But these years do not quite comprise the span of man's life. There are men now living who were born in Venice while it still enjoyed the freedom of 1300 years. There are a few, although but a few, who have seen the last doge bear the ivory sceptre which had passed to his hand from that of Anafesto, and who remember the resolution of the senate, by which they adjourned their meeting " until the French troops had left the city"—the last legal act of government which Venice has ever seen.

But it needs no living memory to recal these ancient glories to the mind of the Venetian; the whole city is their memorial. Their monuments cannot be suppressed without destroying Venice. Every church and every palace tells of former grandeur and greatness. Were the cathedral, the palace, and the prison of the Doges, the campanile, and the column of St. Mark all levelled with the ground, much of Venice would be gone, but even the remains of the city would still bear their memorial of her former glories, which is imperishably engraved upon the very stones of which she is built.

While these memorials remain, can we wonder if the Venetians turn back with passionate and inextinguishable regret to the days when Venice was great and free ? The traveller most alien to Venice in sympathy and feeling cannot approach them without emotion. The senate house appears as if it were ready for the fathers of the Republic to assemble it once more. The chamber of the council seems waiting the entrance of the magistrates, to call before them the suspected traitor ; the hall of audience is swept and garnished for the reception of the envoys of some foreign sovereign. The least imaginative visitor who looks on the dream-like beauty of Venice cannot divest himself of the feeling that he is gazing on a city in a trance. They may surely be forgiven who give themselves up to the impression which everywhere haunts them, which follows them through the palace of the doge, over the waters of the canal, in every church that records the piety of past ages, on the summit of the campanile, and beneath the column of St. Mark, and who, yielding to such influences, refuse to believe that the freedom and glory of Venice are never to be recalled.

Impressions like these are not mere imagination ; they are realities when they influence great masses of men, and whiln they have their hold upon the hearts of the Italians, the peace of Europe never can be secure so long as Austria retains Venice in her grasp.

No transaction recorded in history is less de-

fensible than that by which her title originally
accrued, and history has recorded its irreversible
judgment upon the act by which Venice was
treacherously seized. It boldly stands out on
the historic page an avowed act of plunder, without the semblance of one of those excuses in
which the robberies of power are wont to find
their pretext. The indignation of men has been
abundantly lavished on the conduct of Napoleon.
But of the two parties to that iniquitous spo-
liation the more guilty far was Austria.
Whatever cause of quarrel Napoleon had with
Venice, Austria had none. The soldier of a
revolution that disturbed all ancient landmarks
might have some excuse for a disregard of ancient
right. The power that put itself forward as the
guardian of order and conservatism had none. It
was the demand of Austria that induced Napoleon to become accomplice in her crime. Austria at this hour is in possession of the proceeds
of that crime. With that possession she must
bear in the eyes of mankind its guilt.

From 1797 to 1805 Venice continued annexed to the dominion of Austria. In the
latter year the victory of Austerlitz placed the

cabinet of Vienna at the feet of Napoleon, and the Venetian territory became a part of the kingdom of Italy ; of which Napoleon was king, and Eugene Beauharnois viceroy.

In 1814, upon the downfall of Napoleon's power, the representatives of Europe assembled at Vienna restored Venice to its Austrian masters. These pages are not the place for a discussion of the effects of that settlement, or the influences by which it was accomplished. To make Austria supreme in Italy in order to protect Italy against France — this was the policy which guided the deliberations of the congress. For such a policy there was great excuse in the state of Europe, and in the temper of men's minds. Nevertheless, there were not wanting sagacious men who foresaw in this policy the surest means to that aggrandisement of France, against which it was the great object of the statesmen of the congress to guard. There were those who predicted the evils which Austrian ascendancy would produce to Italy, to Europe, and even to the Papal power. The whole ministerial life of Gonsalvi, after 1815, was occupied in alarmed and anxious watching of

Austrian intrigue, and the Italian arrangements of the congress were not finally carried out without a protest from the Vatican against the policy which sacrificed to German interests the admitted rights of the Pope.

Placed, by the decision of the congress, in possession of Lombardy and Venice, the Emperor of Austria instituted the Lombardo-Venetian kingdom as an act of concession to these territories. This concession was forced on him sore against his will. It was merely a nominal one. The whole system of government was one of oppression. A bitter hatred to their German masters grew up in the hearts of the Italian subjects of Austria. This hatred was reciprocated by their rulers. Disaffection and tyranny re-acted on each other. The government had reason to be stern, because it was dealing with a nation of rebels. The people were justified in their disaffection, because the government oppressed and enslaved them. There are relations between rulers and their subjects, in which good government becomes almost an impossibility. The policy of Metternich was not that which could have solved the problem.

Yet in deep and sullen discontent Venice
appears silently, but with burning indignation in
her heart, to have submitted to the Austrian
yoke.   It was not until the year 1848, that any
serious attempt was made at insurrection.

The accession of the present Pontiff brought
hope and excitement to the friends of Italian
liberty and independence.   The time had come
back when the Church was the ally of freedom,
and the oppressed and enslaved looked for sympathy and protection to the chair of St. Peter.
The impulse given by the liberal and reforming
Pontiff spread like an electric shock throughout
Europe.   Men's minds everywhere were animated with new hopes.   But it was in Italy
that the chords of national life were most power-
fully struck.   Italian princes flung off their sub-
mission to the German under the influence communicated from the measures adopted at the
Vatican.   To this influence the free constitution
of Piedmont is to be traced.   Everywhere the
name of Pius the Ninth became the watchword
of nationality.   The Austrian police throughout Lombardy and Venetia were occupied in
punishing as crimes demonstrations in favour of

the Pope. Austrian troops seized on Ferrara, to overawe the liberal Pontiff. The influence of England was believed to be exerted in favour of Italian freedom. Lord Minto was sent as an envoy of the British Cabinet on a special mission to the Italian States. Himself a member of that Cabinet, he represented the views of his government.* His communications with the Italian sovereigns were directed to induce them to imitate the liberal policy of the Pope. The year 1847 closed full of hope for the Italian cause.

The next year was memorable for the agitations which suddenly shook almost every throne in Europe. Revolutions in Paris and Vienna were the signal for disturbances, more or less serious, in every country. Milan, in a popular insurrection, drove the Austrian garrison away. Charles Albert, in bold defiance, it must be admitted, of all conventional rules and obligations, marched his army to support "his Lombard brethren" against their foreign oppressors. The Italian princes yielded to the popular

* See note at commencement of second volume.

enthusiasm, and seemed in good earnest to support the cause of Italian independence.   Even
the Grand Duke of Tuscany sent his contingent
to the field.   Neapolitan troops were marched to
the defence of Lombardy against the Austrians.
The Papal ministers permitted the Roman battalions to join the national array, and the Pontiff
himself blessed from the balcony of St. Peter's
the soldiers who marched to do battle against
the German.   All Italy seemed on the point
of being united in another "holy league," to
chase the "barbarians" from her soil, with the
Father of the Faithful once more at the head of
the Italian cause.   All that was glorious in the
days of Alexander the Third and Julius the
Second was recalled.   And in the fervour of
their enthusiasm the Italians blessed the day
that had elevated to the tiara a Pontiff who
had all the patriotism and virtues of both,
while he was free from the faults of either.

Such were the hopes and such was the enthusiasm that roused the whole heart of Italy in the
early days of the pontificate of Pius the Ninth.
The history of their disappointment is yet to be

written. That history is far beyond the limit
and object of these few pages.

Venice caught the enthusiasm which pervaded
the land. Then it was that Daniel Manin
arose with an elevation almost as sudden
and marvellous as that of Rienzi. Long che-
rishing the hope of Venetian independence, he
had endeavoured to impress upon his countrymen the lesson that their movements
should be within the law; that even the
limited liberty which had been given them by
the constitution of 1815 supplied them with the
means of obtaining concessions which would
strengthen their country; and that, if that constitution were violated, they must at least place
their oppressors in the wrong. His must have
been a marvellous force of character which, in a
country where the occasions of displaying the
powers of a popular leader were rare and cir-
cumscribed, yet won to him the confidence and
attachment of a whole population.

On the 17th of January, 1848, he was committed to prison for being the author of a petition to one of those assemblies by which Austria
had mocked the wish of the people for repre-

sentative government, a petition in which he used
language the temperance of which in this country
would be said to amount to tameness. During
his imprisonment the news reached Venice that
an insurrection had broken out in Vienna, and
that the Emperor had granted liberal reforms.
Count Palfy, the civil governor, and Zichy, the
military commander of Venice, were both Hungarians, and probably had secret, it may be
to themselves unacknowledged, sympathies with
the oppressed Italians. But without attributing
any influence on their conduct to such motives,
it is very easy to understand that the state of
Vienna paralyzed their exertions. Men could
hardly be expected to use extremities against a
population in revolt, who knew that their sovereign had given way to a popular outbreak in
the capital, and who could not tell how any severe measures against the populace at Venice
would be punished by the new government that
had been, or might be inaugurated at Vienna. In
such a position it is not to be wondered that they
yielded without risking all upon a deadly conflict with the people. On the 17th of March
the populace met in tumultuous assemblage,

and insisted on the release of Manin and his companion Tommaseo. The demand was complied with. Manin, before he could discover the reason of his liberation, was carried, amid the shouts of an excited multitude, from his dungeon first to the governor's palace and then to his home. He could only implore of the people, whatever had happened, to respect the law and observe order. He reached his home exhausted by weakness and excitement, to embrace his family and to sink into a faint.

Five days later the arsenal was in possession of the people. The assassination of the colonel who commanded it is the one solitary crime which the enemies of the Venetian revolution have been able to charge upon it. Of the true nature of that transaction the reader must form his opinion for himself. The arsenal, under Manin's direction, fell into the hands of its assailants. Alarmed and perplexed by this success of the insurgents, Count Palffy gave up Venice without striking a blow. He surrendered his power into the hands of Zichy; and the military commander entered into a formal capitulation, by which Venice was given up to a provisional government, and the Austrian troops evacuated the city.

Manin found himself placed at the head of a provisional government of Venice at the moment when all Italy was rising to assert its independence. The Sardinian and the Tuscan troops alike took the field against the Austrians. Those of the King of Naples marched together with the soldiers of the Pope, while an insurrection in Hungary and a revolution at Vienna appeared to make it impossible for Austria to put forward any strength sufficient to retain her Italian dominions in the face of the determination of the Italian princes and people.

Sterner times soon tried the soul and the courage of the new governors of Venice.

The Italian union did not last long. Hardly had the Papal troops left Rome, when disturbances in that city began to give uneasiness to the Pope, and dissensions between him and his ministers marred the unity which ought to have prevailed. The progress of revolution alarmed those who probably had never been very earnest in the cause of freedom, and they found means of making the Pontiff share their fears. So early as the 18th of April Pius ordered his troops to be recalled; on the 29th he pronounced the allocution, in which he declared war against the Germans abhorrent to his views. The Grand Duke of Tuscany was not slow in ordering back the volunteers whom he had sent, and finally an insurrection in Naples, on the 15th of May, gave the Neapolitan sovereign a reason, or an excuse, for withdrawing his army from the Po.

Charles Albert alone, of all the Italian sovereigns, still actively maintained the national cause; but by the withdrawal of the Neapolitan troops, the national army was so much weakened that the Austrians were able to compel Charles Albert to retreat. On the 8th of August, he signed a capitulation, by which he agreed to withdraw both his army and his fleet from succouring Venice, and to abandon Milan and Lombardy to their fate. It was with difficulty that he escaped being torn to pieces in the streets of Milan.

For a few days before this capitulation, Venice had been placed under the sceptre of Charles Albert. On the 6th, the Venetians had determined to unite with Lombardy and Piedmont,

in one Italian kingdom ; next day the Provisional
Government formally surrendered their power
to the commissioners of the Sardinian king.
Three days were the limit of his sovereignty.
On the 12th, the news of his capitulation had
reached Venice. The royal commissioners abdicated their functions, amid the indignation of
the people, and a triumvirate was formed, of
which Manin was the chief.

Darker days were coming fast on Italy.
The mediation of France and England had been
invoked in vain. The Pope had, in vain, by a
personal appeal to the Austrian Emperor, endeavoured to make peace on the basis of a recognition of Italian independence. Unscrupulous
revolutionists at Rome and elsewhere excited the
people to violence. In the Papal city, Rossi,
the Pope's minister, was murdered, and a popular tumult forced a ministry of ultra-democrats
upon the Pope. At last, in the end of Novem-
ber, the Pontiff fled from the Vatican to Gaeta,
appealing to the great powers, among others, to
Austria, to protect him against the revolutionists
at Rome. In January, the Grand-Duke of Tuscany followed the example of the Pope, and

early in 1849, the separation between the Italian cause and the princes of Italy was complete.

The causes of this miserable result it is not possible in these pages to attempt to trace. They have been referred to the machinations of a party whose real object was to establish a democracy after the example of the French revolution, and who sacrificed to their darling object all hopes of unity among the Italians. Traitors, it has been said, in the guise of patriots, preached rebellion to the soldiers in the camp of Charles Albert in 1848; and the disastrous results of the campaign are attributed to the treachery and divisions of his own army far more than to the force by which he was opposed. If ever the whole truth is known, it will probably be found that most of the scenes of popular violence had their origin in quarters very different from the policy of the cause which they professed to promote. Many contemporary testimonies assure us that the Austrian government was believed to stimulate the more violent democrats to outbursts of passion and to deeds of crime. Unquestionably the most important service that could be ren-

dered to Austria, was to confound the opposition
to her despotism with revolution.   Her best
friends were those who preached republicanism
in the armies of Charles Albert, and infidelity
among the soldiers of the Pope. The deepest
injury to the cause of Italian independence was
to identify it with the theories which, under the
ghastly name of " The Red Republic,'' were
then terrifying Europe with visions of anarchy
and blood.

The ascendancy of Austria became once more
the representative of " law and order." The
republican government of France, that had in
the streets of Paris extinguished " red republicanism" in slaughter and carnage, early in the
year, sent her armies to suppress revolution in
Rome. The year, however, did not pass without another struggle.   It lasted but for a
few days.   The ill-fated Charles Albert staked
his all upon the desperate enterprise, in which if
lofty chivalry and heroic bravery could have re-
deemed the cause of Italy, he would have tri-
umphed.   On the disastrous field of Novara,*
he sought in vain for a soldier's death. De-

* March 23rd, 1849.

serted and traduced by those in whose cause he
had risked his all, he saw, on that field, the
hopes of his life stricken down. On the evening
of the engagement he abdicated his crown, and
retired to hide in solitude and privacy the
agonies of a proud spirit and a broken heart.
Piedmont was compelled to yield to Austrian
demands.

Venice held aloof from the intrigues and the
passions which in other parts of Italy had torn
the national cause. Her citizens appeared ac-
tuated only by a desire to win their freedom
from Austria. In September, 1848, they had
witnessed the departure of the Sardinian fleet,
carrying with them the last of the Sardinian
troops. Every effort was made at the same
time to recall the Neapolitans and Romans who
still lingered in the ranks of the defenders of
Venice as volunteers. The Austrian army was
thus able to take up its position against Venice
without danger of any attack in the rear. But
the winter months passed over without any very
active operations on either side, and the Venetians maintained their attitude of defiant resistance to the force which invested the lagune.

When the spring of 1849 brought accumulated ills to the Italian cause, the spirit of Venice
was still undaunted. The armistice of August
1848 had suspended the movements of the
Sardinian monarch, but left him free to resume
the struggle. But the disastrous campaign
of 1849 reduced Piedmont to virtual subjec-
jection,and the treaty which closed it extinguished
all hope of Sardinian aid. But the enthusiasm
of the Venetians was undismayed. The defeat of
Novara did not quell their courage. When the
ferocious Haynau approached the city, reeking
with the blood of his Lombard massacres, their
answer to his summons was "resistance at any
cost." Two months more brought the news that
the combined armies of Russia and Austria were
crushing the Hungarian patriots with a force
that was irresistible.* All hope from external aid
was gone. They had begun to be vigorously
pressed. Their port was closed by a strict
blockade. A bombardment of the city was
commenced from forts thrown up on the verge

* The Russian troops entered Hungary in May. The
final surrender of Görgey took place on the 13th of
August.

d

of the lagune.   Yet still with a desperate heroism
the citizens refused to yield.   For more than four
months* the siege was protracted.   The horrors
of war and scarcity were aggravated by those
of pestilence.   Even the fall of Rome† seemed
incapable of shaking the determination of
the people.   Men and women were driven
from their homes by the red-hot shot of
the bombardment falling thick and fast in
their habitations.   They moved to the open
streets in the quarters of the town most remote
from the fire of the invader, and shouted death
to those who would propose surrender.   It was
when resistance had been more than proved to
be a useless waste of life, when the means of

* On the 26th of March, immediately after the battle
of Novara, Haynau sent his summons to Venice to surrender. On the 26th of April, he commenced the attack
on Fort Malghera, a defence of Venice on the land side
of the lagune. This fortress did not fall until the 27th
of May. Venice surrendered on the 22nd of August.

During the eighty-five days which followed the
occupation of Malghera by the Austrians, the city was
exposed to the whole fury of their cannonade. The
days were frequently reckoned as the eighty-five
the siege.

† July 4th, 1849.

resistance were, in fact, gone, when almost the last shot had been expended in their arsenal, and scarcely a day's provision remained in the granary,—it was then, and only then, that the personal influence of Manin succeeded in inducing them silently to acquiesce in a capitulation which saved the city from being laid in ruins, and preserved Venice from destruction for the chances and fortunes of a happier day. On the 22nd of August, 1849, the capitulation of Venice was signed; on the 27th the Austrians entered, and a French ship of war carried Manin and his chief associates from those shores which he at least was destined never to see again.

To dwell on the details of this struggle would be to anticipate and weaken the interest of the incidents which the pages of Henri Martin more fittingly record.

Those who feel an interest in watching the struggles of brave men for freedom, will not complain of the minuteness with which those details are narrated. The records of French and English diplomacy, which appear to be derived from the most authentic sources of information, possess for the politician an attraction of another, but not an inferior kind. The attentive observer of the causes which influence the movements of nations, will find in these pages some curious revelations, which throw light upon the history of 1859. Changes of dynasty have, after all, but little effect on the policy of nations. The empire has accomplished for France the designs that were contemplated by the first rulers of the republic. In demanding Savoy as the price of aiding Italy, Napoleon has but carried out the speculations of Lamartine, and the councils of the provisional government, found their realization on the fields of Magenta and Solferino. The policy of our own government, discussed as it is with fairness by the French writer, appears to demand a fuller notice than he has bestowed upon it, and I have elsewhere ventured to offer to the English reader some observations to which the discussion of their policy naturally gives rise.*

It is round Manin himself, after all, that the chief interest of the narrative is centred. Few

* See Introductory note, at commencement of the second volume.

passages in history possess more of the interest of a romance, than that which records the story of his rule over Venice, his guidance of her citizens in their last struggle to be free; the narrative of Henri Martin maintains its unbroken fascination, from the scene in which Manin, beneath the venerable arches of St. Mark, saw the national guards defile before him, and hail him as the liberator of his country; to the description of the last consultation of the Venetian council, when, with reluctance and sorrow, they gave to their dictator the last sad proof of their confidence, by empowering him to surrender the city when he thought fit.

But the story of Manin does not end with that of the Venetian struggle, and a few sentences may be devoted to following the illustrious exile to his last resting-place in a foreign land.

The grandeur of sorrow threw its mournful dignity over his latter years. He left Venice, accompanied by his wife and two children, upon whom he had lavished all the fondness of a heart that was large enough to find room for the tenderest domestic affection, together with passionate love for his country. At Marseilles, where he landed, to seek a shelter in the realm of France, his wife fell a victim to cholera, and the first separation broke up the little household which had been driven from their native land.

A few hundred pounds which, when he left Venice, had been forced on him by his fellow-citizens, from the remnant of their public treasury, constituted all his worldly possessions. The expenses of travelling and illness exhausted his little hoard, and soon after their arrival in Paris, Daniel Manin obtained subsistence for himself and his children, by engaging in the occupation of a teacher of the Italian language. With a stern sense of independence, he rejected all offers of aid from old or new friends, and carried each evening to the humble home he had found for his children, the earnings of his laborious engagements.

A dark shadow rested on that home. His daughter was slowly but surely sinking to the early grave, from which the fondness of a father's tenderest affection could not save her; and in the protracted pain of that suffering child, her father's heart sustained a long martyrdom more

trying far than that of the scaffold or the.
stake.

It is difficult to believe that the exaggerations
of sorrow have not coloured the accounts which
are given us of the attachment that existed
between Manin and his daughter Emilia. But,
after all allowance for the heightened tone in
which the mourner speaks of the daughter of
whom he is bereaved, few tales of human sorrow
make a stronger appeal to the highest and holiest
sympathies of the heart. Even in her childhood,
Emilia Manin had been, in some sense, the companion of her father's thoughts. The interval
is not so wide that separates the thoughts and
feelings of intelligent children from our own.
She grew up with the same passionate attach-
mant to Italy, which was the master feeling of
Manin's heart, and in the instincts of sympathy
the child understood all the exalted patriotism
of the man.

From early years the tenure of her life had
been frail. Her health was preyed on by some
mysterious disease, which is said to have baffled
the skill of the physicians; in all probability the
manifestation of that overwrought texture of the

brain which too often is the penalty of early
intellect, and which not unfrequently attends as
a beautiful but fatal inheritance the children
of those who unite activity of intellect to susceptibility of temperament.

The excitement and the troubles of her early
years were too well calculated to aggravate such
a malady as this. That malady had drawn
close round her father's heart the ties which
bind us most to those who are most dependent
on our love. She was only the more endeared
by her delicacy of frame. Her very sufferings
became sacred, because they were associated
with the cause for which Manin had given up
his all. It was in bitterness and agony of mind
that he wrote on the diary in which he recorded
every day the wasting of her life,

"Alla mia santa martire."

As he saw her pine in the lodging found for her
in the crowded city, he thought how different
might have been her fate if she had never left
the home which he had forfeited, to struggle
with exile, or poverty, or want; that the breezes
of the Adriatic might still have brought health

and vigour to that wasting frame, and the care
of her mother might have stayed the insidious
malady which made

"her little span of life one long disease."

In his watchings of her sufferings, Manin
knew that he was witnessing the slow sacrifice
of his child. Her's was a martyrdom which he
more than shared.

Against all this, and more than this, Manin
nobly struggled. Early in the winter's morning,
in frost, in sleet, or in rain, the ex-dictator of
Venice was seen traversing with weary steps his
long journey to the place of his engagement
through the Parisian streets : he could not afford
to avail himself of any other mode of travel.
Suffering himself from disease of the heart, tortured by anxiety for his son, who, too, began to
pine in the confinement of the city, Manin with
patient industry went through his daily task, to
return with the dusk of the evening to the humble home which his presence still made glad.

"I trembled," he said, "as I approached her
door. I could scarcely bring myself to enter
and look on her suffering frame ; but I knew

my presence brought her joy. When she saw me, her face became transfigured." The gentle sufferer kissed her father's worn hands, and prayed his forgiveness for all the pains her illness cost him.

In January, 1854, death released her from her sufferings. The blow fell heavy on her father's heart, and the residue of Manin's days might be said, with almost literal truth, to have been passed in mourning for his child. Like Edmund Burke lamenting the death of his son, he seemed to think life too short for sorrow for so great a grief, and regarded as taken from devotion to her memory every moment that was withdrawn from contemplation of his loss. He abandoned himself to a grief that found its only alleviation in its own indulgence, a grief like that of " Rachel mourning for her children, and refusing to be comforted because they were not."

The efforts of his friends to console him but drew from him the most touching revelations of the inner sorrow that preyed upon his heart. When pressed to travel in countries he had long desired to see, he answered that he could find no pleasure in the most glorious of nature's

scenes, since his daughter could not be with him
to look upon them too. Through all her sufferings, in one thing he had hoped against hope.
He had cherished the belief that the fond and
gentle spirit that had shared so deeply in the
misery of his sorrows, should one day be glad-
dened by participation in his joy. Even with
the dreams of the patriot, the image of his child
was inseparably associated; and often as he
looked upon her pale and wasted form, and
thought of all she was enduring in his exile, he
sustained himself by looking forward to the
day when she would return with him to Venice,
freed from the dominion of the stranger—when
in the freedom of their country and the tranquillity of their own loved home, by the blue waters
of the Adriatic, and under the sunny skies of
her native land, she might know once more a
happiness that would make amends to her for all.
In the destruction of all these visions his heart
was left desolate. Life had closed upon her
before the dark shadow of her young destiny had
passed away. The hope of the future had lost
to him its power to charm: he had no joy
in the prospect of that brighter day, which could

feeling, Manin did not hesitate to accept the
hope of the realization of Italian liberty, under
the sceptre of the princes of the house of Savoy.

Of this new political creed of Italian patriotism, Manin was the enthusiastic advocate. He
earnestly implored his countrymen to forget all
party differences in its adoption. In following
this course, he had much to learn, and something
to retract. He had always avowed himself a
republican, and had at Venice abandoned power,
rather than serve in a monarchy when the
Venetians placed themselves under Charles Albert. He had opposed the union of Venice
with Lombardy, in a kingdom of Upper Italy,
because such a union would throw back the
prospect of that federation of Italian states
which alone could make Italy a nation. In
1856 he was the prophet of her union, to be
accomplished under the one monarchy of the
Sardinian King.

One of his last acts was to sign, in August
1857, the circular of the "Italian National
Society," an association formed by himself, to
support the house of Savoy, "so long as the
house of Savoy supports the Italian cause."

Of the correctness of his later views, varying opinions will be formed—opinions that involve questions of the deepest interest to Christendom at large. Time alone, perhaps, can bring the solution of these.problems; but whatever be the opinion formed of his wisdom, no one will deny to Manin the credit of being influenced in all the phases of his politics by the one changeless desire to see his country great and free.

He did not live to witness the events of 1859, or hear the sound of those words which rung through Europe, proclaiming, that " from the Alps to the Adriatic, Italy should be free." To use his own words, " Exhausted in a struggle far beyond his strength, he waited with earnest longing the hour of his last and only true repose."

That repose had come to his fevered frame and broken heart nearly two years before the campaign of 1859 had partially realized those visions of Italian freedom, which, in the far-off distance, his prophetic spirit had foreseen. " The great exile of Venice" was resting in a Parisian grave, when France, under the banner of the Third Napoleon, crossed the Alps to give to the

Italian cause that aid which the patriot in his lifetime had so often and so earnestly invoked. On the 22nd of September, 1857, he died in the same room which had been the scene of the long agonies of his daughter. His remains were laid with hers and those of his wife in the vault of a Parisian artist, who extended to the exiles that which has been strangely, but not inappropriately, described as the hospitality of a tomb.

Throughout Italy, but most of all in Venice, the tidings of his death were received with universal mourning. The performance of any funeral service, or of any of those solemnities in which the Roman Catholic church commends the spirit of the departed to God, was forbidden by the Austrian police, who administered a law, under which, to pray for the soul of a patriot is a crime. The service for which his family had asked was interdicted. At the appointed hour crowds of all ranks filled the church, and bowed in silent prayer, while spies and police kept watch for any utterance of the petitions which rose in wordless supplication from every heart. There are tyrants worse than those of old, who deny to their victims even the sad consolation of the expression of their grief.

The anniversary of his death gave occasion to a strange and touching scene. Once more the Austrian government made war on the service for the dead. All priests were menaced with the severest penalties who would dare to offer up a mass, or chant a requiem for the repose of Manin. With the early day a multitude thronged to the church of St. Luc, the parish church of Manin's former home. As they approached, the doors were closed by armed men. All who would attempt to enter were threatened with arrest. The house of prayer, which, according to the pious usage of Roman Catholic countries, is left open for the devotions of all who choose to enter, was shut against the sorrowing crowd who came to pray for their departed chief.

The pious affection of his countrymen found means to baffle even the stern vigilance of the Austrian police; and in a temple which that vigilance had not thought it necessary to guard, was performed the forbidden service that implored peace for Manin's soul.

As the sun went down that evening, an un-

PREFACE

FIRST FRENCH EDITION.

THE grave circumstances in which Europe is now placed have so familiarised the public mind with everything relating to Italy and Austria, that the Author feels it unnecessary to enlarge in a preface on the general considerations which belong to that subject. He confines himself to a statement of the following points :—

1st. That he has selected Manin as the hero of a book on Italy, both as a tribute of affection to the memory of the illustrious dead, and also because this great man who is gone, was among all of our generation who have departed, the most energetic, and the purest impersonation of the principle of nationality and of the fraternal alliance of the Gallo-Latin people.

2nd. That this principle of nationality, denied as it is by cosmopolitan bigots, and by the statesmen of the old diplomacy, is the only principle which can serve, or ought to serve, as the basis of the public law of regenerated Europe.

3rd. That all questions concerning the internal organization, the political constitution, or the social progress of states, while they are parallel to the great question of nationalities, are yet all in the present day subordinate to that question, and are incapable of solution until it is first disposed of.

4th. That the great obstacle to the establishment of free, regular, and peaceful order in Europe, is the existence, in the very heart of Europe, of a machine of centralization entirely artificial, of a great administrative and military monarchy, whose foundations rest on a principle directly opposed to that of nationality. Henceforth it is not Russia which bars the path of progress to Europe,—Russia, which has proved herself to possess the capacity for change,

the power of reforming and altering herself;
but it is the Austrian despotism, incapable, from
its very nature, of change or improvement,
keeping Europe under the system of enormous
standing armies—a system which is destructive
alike to the financial, the political, and the moral
interests of nations, and which permits to
Europe no real peace, but only uneasy armistices.

5th. That this state of things will never
cease until the Italian provinces shall be entirely
and irrevocably severed from the Austrian
Empire—until Italy, which is one single nation,
shall in all its external relations form one single
body politic (whatever may be its internal system), until the federal principle shall have
displaced that of centralisation in that Austrian
Empire, which is only an assemblage of different
nations.

The author, without attempting to point out
in detail the general principles which are the
guiding ones of his thoughts, and of his book—
so far as relates to its immediate object—refers
to a notice recently issued by his publisher,
announcing the approaching publication of this
work :—

"The author wishes to show what manner of men Italy, recovering after three centuries of political death, had once more produced. Without disparaging the value of theoretical discussion, examples, it may always be said, in the words of our great tragic poet,—

'Living examples have far more power.'"

The life of Manin shows what, in our own day, an Italian citizen, an Italian family, an Italian city, can be. We would search far before we could discover in all the rest of Europe, as it is, anything to be compared with the eighteen months of the revolution at Venice. It is not only that no right exists against that right which is here. There are no established facts which can countervail such facts as these. It is for the conscience of Europe to draw the conclusion.

*   *   *   *

HENRI MARTIN.

L

VENICE IN 1848—9,

UNDER DANIEL MANIN.

CHAPTER I.

Treaty of Campo Formio—Origin and Youth of Manin
—Early Projects against Austria—Character and Tac-
tics of Manin—The Scientific Congress and the Rail-
way—Petitions of Manin and Tommaseo—Manin and
Call—Letter from Manin to the Central Congregation
—The Carnival of 1848.

On the 29th of September, 1797, the Executive
Directory of the French Republic addressed the
following instructions to General Bonaparte, its
plenipotentiary in the negotiations for peace
opened with Austria.

"The Minister of Foreign Affairs points out
to you, Citizen-General, the precise limits within

which it is now time to enclose the negociators who, for six months past, have abused our patience. You will find the ultimatum of the Directory in the despatch.

" The Directory desires also to explain the motives which have decided it to take you into its confidence, and to associate you in the deliberation which the glory of the nation demands of it.

"Austria has always desired to establish a footing in Italy, and to gradually absorb all the small states into which that beautiful country is divided, and thus realise its chimera of a Holy Roman Empire.

" Another favourite project with Austria is that of becoming a maritime power.

" It has ever been the interest of France to frustrate the execution of these projects; even under its kings it attempted to rescue Italy from German influence.

" The Cisalpine Republic presents us with the means; but the accomplishment of this great object demands vast resources.

" It is but too evident that if we leave the Emperor Venice, Frioul, Padua, and the territory on the mainland to the banks of the Adige, a river which in its course penetrates into the heart of Lombardy—then Austria will extend its grasp to Naples and Tuscany, to say nothing of Istria and Dalmatia, which, by their intrinsic value and convenience, are of themselves worth more to it than Lombardy itself.

"The Cisalpine Republic, surrounded nearly on every side by that voracious power, will soon become its prey. So far from being able to sustain it, we shall ourselves be expelled from every part of Italy. We shall not have made peace, we shall only adjourn war. In the mean time we give Austria the power of attacking us hereafter with greater advantage; and independently of the disgrace that must attach to our abandonment of Venice, we shall have taken in these negociations the position of the defeated party.

"Let us look to the very worst. Let us, citizen-general! admit a supposition which your own genius and the bravery of your army forbids. Suppose us vanquished and driven out of Italy. In that case we yield only to force and the chances of war, our honour will be preserved, and we shall not have connived at a treachery which could have had no excuse, since it would entail consequences even more disastrous than the most unfavourable chances of war.

" The whole question reduces itself into the consideration, are we willing, or ought we, to give up Italy to Austria ?

" Now, the French Government is not willing, nor ought it to do so. Therefore, it prefers the chances of war to changing a word in its ultimatum, even now too favourable to the House of Austria."

At the moment when this dispatch left Paris, the armies of France, everywhere victorious, were menacing, both on the north and the south, the ancient capital of the House of Hapsburgh, the head-quarters of the counter-revolution. One more effort, and Austria, utterly prostrate, must have signed the terms of peace which France could have dictated at the gates of Vienna. If ever there could be certainty in human affairs, the triumph of France was certain now.

The Executive Directory had given to the hero who, at the head of the army of Italy, fought with one hand, and negociated with the other, instructions conformable with the princi-ples proclaimed by the Revolution on the rights of nationalities. The re-establishment of France within the natural boundaries of Gaul (according to the expression of Richelieu), and the complete emancipation of Italy from the yoke of the foreigner. Such, in pursuance of the policy bequeathed to the revolution by the two great statesmen of the monarchy, was the two-fold basis of the treaty which the Republican government intended to impose upon the House of Austria. But the young General, who in a few short months had surpassed all modern, and equalled all ancient glory, already deemed his destiny too high to be subordinate to any other consideration; and the rights of governments, or even of nations, weighed but little against the absorbing personality of this new Cæsar. True glory called him to Vienna, but he turned away his head; for his eye was fascinated by the glittering phantoms that waved the sceptre of the East on the road to Egypt and India. He feared, also, lest the army of the Rhine, although deprived of its magnanimous Hoche, should reach Vienna before him, and that he might thus see the matchless glory of his Italian war diminished by the participation of others in the final triumph.

He signed the treaty of Campo Formio, which, including but one of the two bases demanded by the Directory, restored the integrity of France at the cost of mutilating Italy,—immolated by the hands of republican France an ancient and illustrious republic—and surrendered to Austria the city of Venice and the greater part of Venetia.

The material advantages accorded to France were very great—but the moral strength of the Revolution was lost by this fatal treaty. The new law of right disappeared, — the republic bartered nationalities as kings had done. Here we may discern the foreshadowing of those gloomy times when the international principles of the Revolution, abandoned by France, would be turned against her. The germ of 1813 was planted in 1797.

The Directory hesitated. If it broke with the man who seemed the incarnation of victory, if it dared to dispense with his sword, and braved his resentment, where could it look for support? Hoche was no more! The Directory sorrowfully ratified this abdication of the new political creed, this denial of the revolution by itself!

The poor opinion entertained of Venice by Europe, at the close of the eighteenth century, had prepared the mind of the French people, perhaps, even of Napoleon himself, for suffering this great iniquity. Not that the Venetian government shocked the imagination so much by its mysterious tyranny, (so fantastically exaggerated in plays and romances), as it excited contempt. Its grandeur had long ago been eclipsed—now its wisdom disappeared. That power which formerly engaged its subjects in action, in the arts, navigation, and war, now appeared as if it knew not how to secure their obedience, except in enervating them by dissolute manners. Effeminacy, falsehood, and corruption, universally prevailed. Nevertheless, when, at the eleventh hour, Venice, at the feet of an inglorious despotism, abjured an independence of thirteen centuries, and became the spoil of the conqueror—there arose a cry of despair from the depths of its heart which made Europe shudder.

A senile and perfidious aristocracy, justly crushed by Bonaparte for being the accomplice of Austria, had been succeeded by a new democracy, under the patronage of France, which now sacrificed it. The old nobility, which had abdicated, and the revolutionary *bourgeois*, its successor, both fell, struck by the same blow.

The regrets of the one, and the lost hopes of the other, blended in the same wail. The grief extended beyond Venice, not only to Italian, but also to Greek and Slavonic Venetia. When the tree had fallen, it was then seen how large and deep were its roots. A lingering decline had not deprived this people of its remembrance of those times when an aristocracy, restraining un-due assumption in its own members, united moderation to strength, and governed its sub-jects with an enlightened gentleness of which Europe presented no similar example. The strength had departed, but the gentleness still subsisted. The Dalmatians buried the banners of the lion of St. Mark beneath the altars of their churches. Venice could not even attempt to defend herself, for Bonaparte had removed her fleet and stores. The Austrians entered the city. The last doge, whose weakness had hastened the calamity, fainted at the moment when he swore allegiance to the new master! The name of that doge was Manin!

This, even in the eyes of those who blamed the victim, was the last sigh of Venice. All became silent. The tomb closed over the Queen of the Adriatic, and the heavy hand of Austria sealed the stone.

For ten years the Austrians had kept guard over the sepulchre, when a child was born, whose destiny it was to recal Venice to life. By a coincidence, in which the ancients would have found mysterious symbols, the future initiator and martyr of a new democratic Venice bore the same name as the last chief of ancient Venice. Although the plebeian infant was a stranger to the downfallen patrician family, he sprung from that powerful Jewish race, which since, little by little, it has ceased to be separated by implacable prejudices from the rest of mankind, has given so many remarkable men of all kinds to Europe. In the course of the preceding century, his family had embraced Christianity; probably under the patronage of the Manin family, whose name it assumed.

The early years of Daniel Manin passed between two revolutions; in which Venice, without at all participating in the events which decided its fate, passed from hand to hand like a corpse. First, the Austrians remained eight years; then, he who had given Venice to them

retook it, this time, áfter entering Vienna. He
kept Venice, and Italy also, to himself. For
another eight years Venice endured this second
master. When the French empire collapsed,
the Austrians returned, and railed against
" French tyranny," in the words "liberty" and
" national independence." *   Then, with a pro-
fusion of those promises which proclaimed
everywhere the great deception of 1815, they
secured the victory of the Holy Alliance over
Napoleon—the triumph of hypocrisy over power.

Milan foolishly trusted to the Austrian's word,
and revolted (1814). Venice, however, remained
passive. The Austrians reinstated and consoli-
dated themselves. German promises had availed
even Germany but very little; they were worth

* See the proclamations of the Archduke John, in
1809 ; of General Nugent in 1813 ; the convention of
evacuation (April, 1814), &c.   "Do you wish to be
Italians once more ?   Unite your strength, your arms,
your hearts, to the generous arms of the Emperor
Francis. He sends a powerful army to Italy, not to
satisfy a vain thirst for conquest, but to secure independence to all the nations of Europe." (Proclamation of the Archduke John.)   "Italians, let our oath
convince you. You will become an independent nation." (Proclamation of General Nugent.),

infinitely less to Italy, which quickly found itself a *conquered*, not a *delivered* country. The people smothered their indignation, which, nevertheless, burned fiercely in their hearts. Still— when in 1820 and 1821, a liberal movement, breaking out in the very bosom of armies, roused all southern Europe into a state of reaction against the deception of 1815—when the constitutional revolt of Naples and Piedmont (so quickly crushed at the time) had for a counter-stroke the agitations of the youth of Lombardy, suppressed and chastised by the atrocious vengeance which consigned the flower of the Milanese nobility to the dungeons of Spielberg— Venice remained unmoved, and appeared to confirm the opinion so generally entertained, that she was lifeless.

But this would at least have been doubted, could the domestic circle of the families of Venice have been penetrated, and the earnest conversations, the thrilling outpourings of pent-up feelings, which left such profound impressions in the hearts of young Manin, and many others who became the patriots of 1848, had been overheard.

All the traditions and fervour of the Revolution revived within those closed doors. Manin's father, a distinguished lawyer, with his
preceptor, the learned and enthusiastic Foramiti,
philosophers and democrats of the republican
period, inveighed unceasingly against both Austrians and French. The elder Manin entertained
the most implacable animosity against Napoleon,
because he had not emancipated Italy, and restored Poland. The youth grew up amid these
secret exciting scenes, and matured his patriotism by the warmth of these hidden fires. In
this domestic club his policy imposed moderation on his elders. From their passionate
outpourings he gathered ideas. To an active,
practical mind, he united the deepest sensibility,
and the love of a simple, well-regulated life; and
the same love of order in the domestic circle,
that he afterwards displayed in governing the
State. Yet, by a singular contrast, in a nature
constituted for thinking, not dreaming, apparently so happily balanced—beneath the ardour
of his soul and the charming vivacity of his
nature, there appeared a singular vein of melan-
choly. Overflowing with energy, yet he became

weary before acting.   Many years afterwards,
he wrote: " The act of living, in a healthy person, considered in itself, ought to be a pleasure:
but to me, from my very childhood, it has always been a painful effort.   I always feel weary."
Morbid principles disturbed this fine organi-
sation from the first, and a constant struggle
against physical suffering was not one of the
least features of his heroism.

A marriage of affection cast some rays of
sunshine over the path of his youth.   United
without fortune, at the early age of twenty-one,
to a noble-hearted woman, he had to labour
hard for the support of his family.   His father's
example, and the judicial and historical tenden-
cies of his mind, had drawn him to the study of
jurisprudence, with which he united a profound
study of philology.*   He became Doctor of
Laws at seventeen, a fact almost unparalleled in
the history of Universities.   He translated the
great French work by Pothier, on Roman law,

* At the age of fifteen he translated the apocryphal
book of *Enoch* from the Hebrew (1820 or 1821).   From
1829 to 1830, he was engaged in compiling a Dictionary
of the Venetian dialect.

while waiting his coming of age, when access to
the paternal profession would be open to him.
In 1830, he established himself at the town of
Maestra, at the entrance to the Lagoons, as an
advocate—an advocate under Austrian rule, without
the power of pleading at the bar of any court—who
could be consulted only in civil cases, for in criminal cases the interference of advocates was not
permitted.   Austria feared both thought and
speech. In this nineteenth century, it adopted the
procedure of the Inquisition—a procedure without the confrontation of witnesses, without
pleadings or publicity.   Compared with the
régime of Francis II., the despotism of Napoleon would have been almost liberty.

The young advocate, with more discrimination
than his father, knew how to distinguish the
difference between the German system and the
French code: between the Gallo-Italian administration of Eugene Beauharnois, and the
cold-blooded system of draining Italy, for the
benefit of its Germanic provinces, practised
by Austria.   Lombardo-Venetia, which in
superficial area formed the eighteenth part
of the Austrian empire, and held one
seventh of its population, had to sup-

port one-fourth of its burdens! The former
taxes were doubled: though nominally 28 per
cent. instead of 16, they were actually 32.*
Almost every office was bestowed upon foreigners. Italian producers and consumers were
sacrificed to a protective system, intended to
benefit the Austrian producer. Milan and Venice were sacrificed to Vienna and Austria.
Apparently there was a pure, but well regulated
monarchy, with some popular institutions, but
in reality an arbitrary police government, ending
in those mysterious prisons which the *good Emperor Francis* governed in secret. Abandoning
the whole government to Metternich, he devoted
himself specially to the torture department.†

Such was the fate of Austrian Italy generally,
but Venice was not even on a level with the
common oppression ; it was far below it. It was
worse treated than Lombardy, because it was
less feared. It laboured under the contempt

* Montanelli, *Memoria sull' Italia*, vol. 2, ch. xxxv.
† See the revelations in the Memoirs of Andryane,
on the torments of hunger inflicted under the personal
superintendence of the Emperor Francis II., on his prisoners, *for the good of their souls.*

inspired by the last days of its aristocracy, in the lowest grade in the scale of servitude. The strong practical sense of the Venetian populace, which protected them against vain and idle murmurings, contributed to conceal the vast strength that lay concealed beneath this silence. The flame which had broken out in 1797, although then instantly betrayed and gagged, still smouldered in this democracy. Its chief element was the body or order of Secretaries, which, under the old government of Venice, had filled many subaltern, and a few higher, offices, and had given the plebeian masses some initiation into public affairs. In France, the revolution of 1830 had overthrown the establishment of 1815. The commotion it excited was much more formidable than that of 1820. It shook Europe, from the Pyrenees to the Vistula. At the beginning of 1831, it made a second effort, when the Romagna, Bologna, and the duchies of the Po revolted.

Daniel Manin kept aloof from a secret society formed at Venice. His instinct and reason were always averse to such modes of political action. But believing that the hour had now arrived, he conceived the bold project of seizing upon the arsenal, and, in concert with three of his friends, among whom was the devoted and loyal Degli Antoni, he drew up a proclamation, intended to excite the people to revolt.

The reverses of the neighbouring provinces prevented the Venetian insurrection. The power which had arisen out of the Revolution of July in France, proclaimed the principle of non-intervention, and in the case of Belgium, had caused it to be respected. But it was not respected in Italy. At the present crisis Austria interfered in the Roman States, and in the Duchies. The rising was quickly stifled in blood, and the hopeful visions of deliverance harshly dispelled.

The authors of the proclamation were not discovered. The young advocate withdrew within his private sphere, and devoted himself to peaceful pursuits. Seven years later, having become a mature man, we see him quit his obscurity and throw himself desperately into the discussions on the projected lines of railways.

Had he then become converted to the utilitarian spirit of the age? to the materialism of

cosmopolitan industry, which new sects set up
as religion ?   He, so indifferent to the pleasures
and vanities of fortune; he, independent, and
to a rare degree even for Italy, of those factitious
wants with which Italy is less acquainted than
France ?   No, he is not changed; but his political genius has developed itself, and suggested
to him a masterly evolution, a profound and
sagacious plan of political agitation. No tyranny
but what leaves some door open to liberty;
through that the square must be entered.   No
despotism but what has its laws, however bad
they may be ; these laws must be used as wea-
pons to fight with.   The positions which cannot
be turned must be carried.   The people must
be accustomed to acting in concert, whatever be
the immediate object, or however foreign it may
appear to political liberty ; by this practice public
spirit may be regenerated.

Daniel Manin has been compared with
Daniel O'Connell, but only by those who understood neither.   Their measures, but not their
aims, were similar.   O'Connell did not pretend,
like the *United Irishmen* of 1798, to separate
Ireland from Eng and ; he did not believe Irish

independence possible, nor, perhaps, desirable.
In combatting the English government with
English laws, he aspired only to secure for the
Irish equality with the English in the free
British Empire; always an *agitator*, he was
never a revolutionist. Manin took, he was
obliged to take, a different view. He had not
to do with a small nation, annexed bodily to a
larger one, with which it claimed equality in
the eyes of the law. Manin, the citizen of a
dismembered country, the severed portions of
which wished to be joined together again, did
not desire to conquer a place in a free nation
for his countrymen. The great bureaucratic
and military machine called Austria, is neither
free, nor a nation; he wished to make use of
that semblance of legality which Austria is
forced to acknowledge, to show that Austria
neither wished nor was able to respect the very
laws it had made; that its domination was
incapable of amelioration; that for Italian misery
there was no remedy except in Austria's downfall. Manin was agitator in order to become
revolutionist.

But he was a revolutionist of a very rare

kind, and some remarks are necessary to explain
his conduct.   On the one hand, he was revolutionist from reason and feeling, not from temperament.   In the highest degree a man of
action, but of regulated action ; a man of order,
in the truest sense of the word ;* an essentially
humane man, he detested tumults, seditions,
and outrages, as practices pernicious to the
morality of a people, and as causing a useless
effusion of blood.   But against foreign tyranny
he approved only of the rising of the masses,
and not of partial and abortive scuffles and
émeutes.   On the other hand, this man, who,
according to his own testimony, acted only
upon inspiration ; who in action was everything
by enthusiasm, and nothing without it.   It is
true that enthusiasm never quitted him during
action.†   This man had, in deliberation, the

---

* "Against disorder I feel a repulsion not only of
reason but of instinct, the same as I feel against everything contrary to the laws of harmony, a deformed face,
a discordant sound."—*Manuscript Notes of Manin.*

† And the weakness that followed was due to physical
causes. "When my faculties are in a state of exaltation,
they sometimes produce uncommon effects; if the ex-

soundest judgment, the clearest views, the most
imperturbable coolness, and a mind completely
inaccessible to every illusion. He appreciated,
as the most disinterested stranger would have
done, the reality of the facts, the amount of
obstacles, the greatness of the material forces of
Austria, the defects of character, situation, resources, and experience which rendered the
united action of the Italian populations, and the
success of this action, so difficult. He did not
believe an Italian revolution possible, except by
a revolution in France,* or in Germany itself.

In awaiting the chances of the future, he

altation fails, I feel myself inferior to the commonest
man, incapable of doing what can be accomplised by
the most mediocre."

* He judged by what really was, not by what might
be ; upon the policy adopted by Louis Philippe, not by
the different policy which was more than once advised
this Prince by his own family. In 1847, a General,
animated with very French notions, came from Africa
to see the king :—" A political crisis is imminent in
France; a great diversion from without can alone avert
it, and strengthen the dynasty. Make war upon Austria,
and throw the army of Algiers into Italy." The King
treated the General as a madman, and sent him back to
his post.

rejected immediate insurrection as a crime, which would only cause the sacrifice of valuable lives; but at the same time, as before stated, he did not believe that legal opposition would obtain a real national reform from the ruling foreigner. Will it be surrounded by impossibilities ? No; for he has not named a fixed day for the revolution; and time may and will modify the terms of the problem. If he cannot make a revolution, he will at least prepare the way for one. Should revolutions occur in France and Germany, then one in Italy would be possible. But while waiting for movements in other countries, legal opposition will constantly serve to train the people, and to obtain some concessions which will strengthen public spirit without satisfying it. If, contrary to all expectation, against all appearances, Austria honestly grants a constitution—a national reform (we shall see hereafter what was meant by that), it shall be accepted loyally, and we shall trust to the force of events to perfect, some day, freedom by complete independence.

Without this clue to the policy of Manin, it would be impossible to apprehend one of the most

original traits of his character : the extraordinary
mixture of ability, equal to that of the most
profound diplomatists of ancient Italy, with a
rectitude and frankness that never left him, even
in the presence of stranger or enemy. Reserving only his inmost feelings for the future
and final end, he always spoke the present truth
to his adversaries, the truth upon facts, the immediate aim of his actions.

We shall soon see him at work in open political action.

We need not repeat the debates on the Lombardo-Venetian railway, or on the quarrels of
Venice and Trieste ;* debates in which the Austrian government had the Viennese bankers and
the Trieste armourers for auxiliaries, and associates in quarrying Italy.† The Cabinet of Vienna

* M. de Bruck, who must be taken as the most characteristic representative of a new Austria, and who has
contributed so much to transform the aristocratic despotism of Metternich inte a semi-bourgeoise despotism,
was at this period director of the Austrian Lloyd's at
Trieste, and made a conspicuous figure in the fight
against Italian interests.

† They were not its only associates; the Austrian
aristocracy employed another process to pump money

concluded by arbitrarily dissolving the Italian Railway Association; but Manin and his friends had attained their object; they had united the Milanese nobility and the Venetian citizens in a common cause; two political classes were sketched out in the two centres of Lombardo-Venetia, and a new Venice, raising the tomb of the old, was dimly foreshadowed.

Yet everyone did not view matters in this light: the apparent calmness of the Venetian people, amid the fermentations around them, looked like apathy in the eyes of the uninitiated. Venice had stifled the cries of its heart before the martyrdom of many of its children; the brothers Bandiera and Moro were immolated on those Neapolitan shores, which were continually washed with the purest blood of Italy. Pius IX. had ascended the Holy Chair. Then came

out of Italy; this was the famous lotteries of Vienna, which found so many dupes in Europe. The administration of the lotteries received payment in Augustine florins, but paid in Vienna florins, worth much less than the others, and this without notifying foreigners. (*See the Histoire de la Republique de Venice sous Manin,* par A. de la Forge, vol. i. p. 18.)

1846 and 1847, those years of feverish illusions, in which the whole peninsula dreamed of, and attempted, for the last time, the alliance of liberty and nationality with the pontifical royalty of Rome. A solemn proof, the more decisive, seeing that it was attempted with sincerity on either side, that it failed not through the ill-will of men, but from the nature of things. In the passionate fervour of those regions of Italy which were not in the occupation of the foreigner, harsh words were cast upon Venice, "accustomed and resigned," they said, "to the Austrian yoke." The ardent members of the secret societies and conspiracies went so far as to accuse Manin and his friends of opening a mischievous outlet for the public sentiment, and of sanctioning the Austrian dominion by making war upon it with its own laws.

Manin, indifferent to imputations which attacked only himself, was touched to the heart by everything which attacked his country, yet in no respect modified his policy, convinced that it was the best; but he was roused to renewed activity. The transit of the Overland Indian Mail, which Venice attempted to dispute with Trieste,—the cholera, which Italy considered

contagious, solely because Germany pronounced
it non-contagious—the idea of an Italian Customs' League—that of an agrarian association
(assurance society among landowners) of the
Venetian Provinces—the scientific congresses,
in fact, every thing presented to Manin materials
of action, or of opposition. The Italian Scientific
Congress, which assembled at Venice in Novem-
ber, 1847, enabled him to loosen the tied tongue
of this generation, which, in the words of the
historian,* "had succeeded the eloquent generations of ancient Venice." In the skill with which
he directed the discussions of the congress and
mingled politics with every economical question,
we can see the manifestation of the statesman
under the guise of the tribune.†

  * M. A. de la Forge.
  † A characteristic anecdote redoubled the popularity
of Manin during these intervals. In M. de la Forge's
book (v. i. p. 106), we read the history of Padovini,
the poor infirm workman who had placarded on the
public square his complaint against the government,
which, he said, left him to die of hunger. He was in hopes
they would give him his bread in a prison : they gave
it him in a madhouse. Manin employed himself with
his usual perseverance and vigour, to put a stop to this

Still, he did not yet clearly understand himself. "If our country were free," his wife said
to him one day, "you should be minister!"—
"God protect me from it," he replied, "my
vocation is opposition." Having no desire for
power, he thought he had no aptitude for it.
Afterwards, when in exile, when pressed to dis-
tract the torments of his recollections by writing
them: "I cannot write," he replied, with one of
those sudden and charming smiles which sometimes illumined his usually gloomy countenance,
"I don't know how to do anything—I am good
for nothing, except to govern men."

There was truth in this sally: God had placed
the sign of command on his brow.

iniquity. "The physicians," he wrote in his petition
to the government, "acknowledge the man is sane;
but they dare not set him at liberty, fearing it
would be contrary to the views of the police and government. For my part, I have a better opinion of the
government and the police. I do not admit that they
create madmen by decrees. If Padovini is culpable
there are the laws." Count Palffy, the Governor of
Venice, impatient of his obstinacy, said, "We must release Padovini from the madhouse, and put Manin in
his place." The people of Venice thought differently.

During these intervals, he threw his whole
soul into a page worthy to be remembered,
composed on the occasion of a · paper written
by Count Jablonski, a relation of the Governor
of Venice, in which he exhorted the Italians to
have resignation : Manin's few lines might serve
as an antidote to a more illustrious work—to
that book, so touching, so reverent, but so
dangerous, of Pellico !

RESIGNATION.

" It is the fashion to preach resignation.

" I distinguish two kinds of resignation ; the
one virtuous and manly, the other cowardly, and
worthy only of fools.

" The strong man, when overcome by misfortune, seeks the means of remedying it.
Does he find any ? In spite of difficulties, he
applies himself to the task, excited, cheerful, and
vigorous, full of energy and pertinacity. It is
only when he is certain that no remedy exists,
that he becomes resigned. This is manly resignation.

" The coward, when misfortune overtakes
him, allows himself to be cast down, and seeks

no means of remedying it. However spontaneous and easy relief may present itself to his mind, he attempts nothing, he wishes neither to trouble nor expose himself—he is resigned: this is the resignation of the fool.

" Therefore, resignation is virtuous and manly under evils manifestly without remedy; it is cowardly and stupid when we can in any way free ourselves from these evils.

" In the individual, resignation may often be virtuous; in a nation, it is perhaps never so, for the misfortunes of a nation are seldom irremediable.

" To overcome the misfortunes of a nation, we can employ the whole intellectual, moral, and physical power of all its citizens; and if the generation which commences the generous task does not succeed in accomplishing it, other generations follow, who will attain success; for nations never die.

" This is the reason why those who advise resignation to nations, advise cowardice, and the nations which become resigned are cowards."

Circumstances prevented the publication of

this remarkable effusion,* but without being acquainted with it, Venice and Italy soon applied its principles.

Manin was more and more setting them the example. The laws of Austria supplied still a weapon more formidable to the government of the foreigner, than any which Manin had yet employed, but it was one to the wielding of which, the consciousness of power and support was essential. Besides the existence of judicial investigation, there was under the German dominion some appearance of political liberty. In 1815, under the influence of the 20th March, Austria had granted central and provincial assemblies to Lombardo-Venetia. But in that system of universal deceit, the secret instructions from Vienna practically annulled everything which seemed liberal in theory. The Congregations were never anything more than the vain shadows of national representation. Nevertheless, the law, the *external* law, gave them one power—that of recording their sentiments. Manin, at the very time he

* This essay, found among the papers of Manin, was published in the Turin *Indipendente* by M. Ernest Legouvé.

was writing in the *Guide,* a comparative study
between the judiciary laws of Austria and those
of ancient Venice, much less harsh in reality,
openly advised his fellow-citizens to render every
obedience to the political laws.

Milan preceded Venice. On the 9th of
December, 1847, Nazari, deputy of the central
Lombard Congregation, made a motion to represent the griefs of the country to the imperial
government. Not one among the deputies of
the Venetian Central Congregation ventured to
follow his example. Manin alone, as a private
individual, signed a petition to this assembly,
with the same object (21st December). "The
Congregations,"* said he, "have never been
the interpreters of our wants or wishes—their
silence has arisen from a fear of displeasing the
government; but this fear is unjust, and injurious: for it is unjust and injurious to suppose
that the government has granted to this king-

ᵣ * These Congregations or assemblies were elected by
the communal councils, and composed partly of nobles,
and partly of landowners. The government reserved to
itself the *veto* on the elected, and the nomination of the
presidents

dom a derisory national representation, that it
deceived, and still deceives, this country and
Europe, in making laws which it does not wish
to be observed, and in prosecuting and punishing
those who intend observing them."

The whole epistle is written in this clear,
brief, nervous, axiomatic style, which character-
ises the iron pen of Manin.   Under the most
strictly legal forms he breathes a bitter irony.
"He has done his duty," said his wife, upon
hearing that the petition was presented, "come
what may."

Everyone felt that he was engaged in a great
struggle.   All Venice left its name at Manin's.
Milan sent its deputy to congratulate him.   On
the morrow of Christmas Day, upon the re-
opening of the *Fenice* theatre, Verdi's *Macbeth*
was given.   When the chorus commenced the
revolutionary strain—

> "La Patria tradita a serger t'invita,
>   Fratelli, corriamo la patria a salvar !"*

the whole audience rose and joined in the chorus.

* "The country betrayed invites thee to rise. Brethren, hasten to save the country."

Dumb Venice spoke at last. It wrote also! Every wall, not of Venice only, and the Venetian cities, but of the smallest villages, was covered with *Viva Pio Nono!* which for the time seemed equivalent to *Viva l'Italia!* with this was frequently mingled the menacing inscription *Morte ai Tedeschi!* (Death to the Germans!)

But the legal campaign was not yet concluded. Manin had not yet exhausted his part of *advocate*. The 30th of December saw a second petition follow the first. It was dictated by the eloquent poet and politician, Tommaseo, one of the most eminent men of Italy. It attacked a special grievance—the censorship of the press. The entire literary club (*Ateneo*) of Venice signed the petition, after a brilliant discourse from the poet, who, developing the system of Manin, showed that the law of censorship, as liberal in theory as censorship could be, was not only aggravated and perverted, but continually violated by the arbitrary acts of the administration.

The news that every day reached Venice, added to the excitement. Italy was convulsed from the Alps to the shores of Sicily. Not-

withstanding the ill success of the risings at
Reggio and Messina, in spite of the sad fate of
Romeo, sacrificed like the brothers Bandiera,—
the waves of revolution reached the Two
Sicilies. The governments of Rome, Tuscany,
and Piedmont, appeared successively drawn into
a liberal and national course. At Milan an
address was circulated among the youth of all
classes, inviting the people to follow the example
of the American colonists, who proscribed the
use of tea, to avoid paying taxes to England,—
" renounce tobacco, avoid voluntary taxation."
The government responded by calling in all its
soldiers on furlough, by circulating the report
that it was the factious spirit of the aristocracy
which obliged Austria to levy so many men and
raise so much money to defend itself, and by
endeavouring to incite in Lombardy ideas of
communism and a division of land, in order to
arm class against class. This " *Gallician*"*
policy had fortunately little or no effect upon
the people.

Sanguinary collisions took place; as the
peasantry could not be excited, the soldiers were
let loose. From the 1st of January, 1848, the

* See note at end of volume.

populace had adopted a password forbid-
ding smoking in the streets. On the
3rd, the Austrian soldiers walked about in
groups with cigars in their mouths. Collisions
ensued between these armed men and the unarmed crowd. Then the whole garrison was
called out to disperse the people with violence.
The tumults did not, however, amount to a
revolt, as anticipated and desired by Radetsky,
the commander-in-chief, who, it is said, asked
for " thirty hours of carnage for thirty years of
tranquillity." The viceroy, the Archduke Regnier, " on the contrary, trembled and addressed
soothing proclamations to his *dear Milanese*."
The incidents of Milan were repeated in the principal cities of Lombardy.

At Venice, meanwhile, the Provincial Congregation, upon the proposal of Mocenigo, invited the Central Congregation to adopt Manin's petition of the 4th January. Next day,
while the Central Congregation was in deliberation, the Director-General of Police, M. Call,
of Rosenberg, sent for Manin. Fifteen days
previously, upon the petition being presented,
the Governor, Palffy, had said, that with regard
to Manin, one of three things must be done:

he must be put into a prison or a madhouse,
or at least interdicted from following his profession of advocate. The director of police
assumed a very different demeanour; he treated
Manin with respect; admitted that there were
abuses which needed reform, and appealed to
him by his love for his country to use his influence to prevent order being disturbed. This
was at once to officially recognise this influence,
and to render the man who possessed it responsible for events. Manin firmly maintained his
position. He protested his opposition to outbreaks
of physical force. " To prevent disturbance," he
said, " no means are so good as legal agitation ;
it opens a regular outlet to excitement."—" The
government cannot accede to a demand for reform while the agitation continues."—" The agitation will never cease until reforms are made.
The government must grant many, and do so
quickly, and at once announce its intention of
doing so. I hope that it will comply with the
wishes of the country." The director replied,
" It is our duty to do so. I shall write to that
effect to Vienna."

They parted on the best of terms, but the
Venetian had as much confidence in the Austrian

as the latter had intention of keeping his word.
The Central Congregation having adopted Manin's petition, Count Palffy, the Governor of
Venice, President of the Congregation, to whom
belonged the privilege of forming the commis-
sions, appointed such members as were the
most strongly opposed to reform, on the commission charged with making the report, and of
acting in concert with the Lombard Congregation.   Manin repeated to him in writing everything he had said to the Director of Police, and
thanked the Central Congregation in a letter,
which is an important political document (8th
January).

He maintained the principle that it is not
only a right, but also a duty, to disobey unpublished laws, and all those secret instructions
which paralyze valid laws.   "The constitutive
laws given to this kingdom in 1815," he said,
"have never been observed ; it will no longer
suffice to put them in operation, but you must
impart to them at once all the progress of which
they contained the germ, and which would have
become developed during two-and-thirty years.
The Lombardo-Venetian kingdom must be a

national and Italian kingdom, with a viceroy
and ministers independent of the Cabinet
of Vienna, and responsible to the Emperor
alone; there must be an Italian army, Italian
finances, except a fixed contribution to the
general expenses of the Austrian empire; a
diet of the kingdom voting the laws and
taxes, elected on the broadest basis, and deliberating publicly,* communal liberty, public
and oral legal proceedings, a legal and no
longer an arbitrary police, liberty of the
press, a civic guard, annexation to the Italian
Customs' Union (proposed by Pius IX.), ad-
mission of the Jews to civil rights,† abo-

* "I demand publicity of the debates, because I
believe publicity necessary in all things, but especially
in bodies representative of all classes; the influence of
public opinion excites them to do their duty, and the
public, while present at the debates, is taking lessons in
political science, and learning how to manage commercial, provincial, and national affairs, and to worthily
exercise, on occasion, the functions of elector and elect."
—(Examination of the 19th February, 1848.)

† He prepared public opinion for this reparative
measure by suggesting to Tommaseo, whose fervent
Christian convictions were well known, to write a pam-
phlet in favour of the Jews.

lition of fiefs, and a general revision of the laws."*

Austrian Italy could not demand less, without renouncing all right to be Italian, but this *less*, Austria being what she is, could she grant it? We think not, and Manin thought so too. Essentially, then, it signified that re-reform by Austria was shown to be impossible, and revolution necessary.

Meanwhile Manin, as he wrote to his friends in the provinces, took for his motto *legality, publicity ;* and, as he had promised the representative of Austria, he dissuaded them from any kind of violence, opposition, or secret plotting ; but at the same time he continued to exhort the young men to familiarize themselves with the use of arms, too much neglected at Venice ; as for himself, he appropriated his last savings

* In a petition in support of Manin's letter, one of the most eminent men of Venice, the advocate Avesani, who aided the tribune to raise a subscription for the families of the victims of Milan, remarked that a very great part of what Manin demanded—an Italian ministry, Italian army, Italian finances, public trials—had existed under the despotic empire of Napoleon.— (14th January.)

to the purchase of three fowling-pieces. * He
foresaw, however, other perils than those of a
conflict.   After a few days' hesitation, the
authorities at length made their decision.   On
the 18th of January, before daybreak, the whole
garrison was on foot, Manin and his worthy
ally were arrested : Manin was conducted to that
famous prison of Venice in which so many
illustrious men have been incarcerated.

At the moment when Manin was thus suddenly removed from a feverish activity to a
repose enforced by violence, he had exhausted
all his strength ; while for many years he had
accumulated the constantly increasing occupations of politics upon the labours necessary to
the support of his family, he suffered from disease of the kidneys, which tormented him almost
to death, without a single complaint ever escaping
his lips to betray his sufferings to his most intimate friends.   To so many pains and afflictions
there was added a crowning cause of physical
exhaustion and intense mental suffering, the
cruel and incurable malady of a tenderly loved
daughter, near whose side he shared the sad

* A. de la Forge, t. i. p. 159.

vigils of the mother, to avoid leaving the child
to the mercenary care of strangers. He succumbed under the burden; and the Austrians,
in condemning him to involuntary inaction, perhaps saved his life—certainly they helped to
recruit his strength for fresh and greater efforts.*

His adversaries, who had seized his person,
reckoned upon rendering such new efforts impossible. At the very time that two indict-
ments against both the prisoners were entrusted
to two counsellors of the criminal court of Venice, the Director-General of Police, the M. de
Call who had had so courteous an interview
with Manin, sent the following note to the President:—

"In the event of an acquittal inform me
immediately, and do not set them at liberty."

The whole system of the government is com-
prised in these few words : justice was a sham ;
the police was the beginning, as it was the end
of everything.

Proceedings against Manin were commenced
on the 21st of January. The impassioned his-

* A. de la Forge, t. vi. p. 172.

torian of *Venice under Manin* has already exhibited the extraordinary character of the exami-
nations, in which the magistrate, a kind and
honest Italian, unwillingly obeyed the foreigner,
and trembled for the prisoner, who did *not*
tremble!—where the young auditor (*ascolante*)
who assisted the magistrate, concealing the
Italian tricolour near his heart, devoured every
word that fell from the prisoner: where the prisoner dictated to the usher of the court, not the
words of explanation or defence, but a broad
exposition of his conduct, a manifesto, and an
ultimatum to the government that prosecuted
him. Not only he said nothing but what was
strictly true, but he spoke the whole truth: all
the police of the world could not have discovered
another incident to add. "I have believed, and
I still believe, that bad actions and vicious passions alone have need of mystery. Therefore I
have ever abhorred mystery. I have always
freely and publicly spoken my opinions upon
every subject, to everybody, fearless of spies, but
going into their presence as a means of diffusing
my ideas, as channels through which the voice

of the people might reach the ears of authority."*

On these points, then, he was perfectly candid. The skill of his statement consisted in
the distinction which he maintained between
the local and the imperial government; between
the sovereign and his agents; between authentic
law and special instructions. He met his adversaries with their own monarchial principles,
according to which the sovereign alone can
make laws, and abrogate, modify, or interpret
them; which deprive instructions, ministerial
or other notifications, of all their value, if they
alter the laws. "The day in which I cast
into the fire all modifications not emanating
from the sovereign, that will be the day of deliverance."

He showed h's skill, therefore, in assuming
that the monarch would render justice, and con-
cede liberty and nationality, in which case Manin
went so far as to speak of the external services
the Italian army might render to the empire,
and of the strategetic interest which Austria
would have in the railway from Verona and the
Tyrol, so much demanded by Lombardo-Venetia;

* Examination of 17th February; MS.

but his " *Sinon non* " emphatically preserved
the dignity of the citizen.

Amid these scenes of learned political encounter, we meet with a touching episode. When the
magistrate demanded of the prisoner an explanation of one of the letters seized at his house, this
man, just now so strong, melted into tears. It was
a letter from Paris, containing a magnetic consultation on his daughter's malady. After having
vainly tried all the resources of medicine against
the terrible nervous affection which tortured
this good angel, as the unhappy father called
her, he had recourse to a Venetian magnetizer,
and then consulted a celebrated " medium" at
Paris. But the magnetic action, instead of
calming the nervous crisis, increased its violence ;
and the poor child, in the acute torment of her
sufferings, implored to be delivered from the
fluid which whirled, as she described it, through
every organ of her frame ! The father, in his
despair, regarded as a crime his unsuccessful
efforts to mitigate her sufferings.

Manin exhibited these contrasts in his whole
life : invincible strength in public, tenderness
and suffering in private.

At this time a new blow fell upon the sorely tried house. On the 23rd of January, Manin wrote to his wife and children a letter filled with expressions of tenderness and heroic pride. " If you continue to be strong and courageous, these will be the happiest days of my life. . . You will find a few pieces of gold in one drawer, a little silver in another. . . . If this affair lasts long, we must think of providing for you in some way. Love one another, my angels : be resigned, that is sufficient."

In this letter he enquired if his sister was in Vienna. He had at Trevisa a younger sister, Ernesta Viezzoli, who, by the nobility of her mind, was worthy of being his sister. A fearful sight, the murder of a citizen by Austrian soldiers, had given a severe shock to the health of Madame Viezzoli. The news of her brother's arrest killed her. Her death drew from the prisoner the only cry for vengeance that ever escaped from his merciful soul.

Manin's wife and friends shewed themselves worthy of him. They did as much as he permitted them to do. A few days after his arrest, his wife, directed by the advocates, his colleagues, addressed to the Director-General of the Police, and to the Criminal Court, a twofold request to obtain, conformably to the law, his release upon bail; seeing that he had been arrested as a simple measure of police policy, and not upon "legal evidence," nor upon a previous decision of the criminal authority. The request offered as bail, the signatures of all the notable persons of Venice, the *podesta* (mayor) at the head. The patriarch was almost the only one who refused his signature (24th—27th January). A similar request was sent in behalf of Tommasseo.

The police would not, the tribunals dared not, do right.* The police prevaricated; the councillor had engaged the police to make Teresa Manin understand "that the case in which he was instructed concerning her husband, *was not pending before any of the judicial authorities.*" The police replied to Signora Manin, that *during the deliberations pending before the judicial authorities*, the Director-

* We say "tribunals;" because the Venetian magistrate referred to the superior tribunal of Milan.

General did not believe himself authorized to accede to her request (2nd February).*

The sensation created by this denial of justice was immense. The entire population, attired in mourning, defiled along the Riva dei Schiavoni, before the windows of the prison; every head was uncovered. The advocates in a body took charge of the office of Manin, so long as his captivity lasted; an artisan, one Toffoli, a tailor, solicited the honour of providing for the prisoner's family: a host of similar offers followed. Manin thanked his fellow citizens, but preferred availing himself of another resource, the reprinting of a little treatise on Venetian jurisprudence. Permission was asked; the local censor declared that he was obliged to refer to Vienna: finally, upon the renewed applications of the prisoner, he verbally replied, that permission was granted, on condition that there should be no advertisements, or notices in journals, or subscription lists; in fact, that the author should make no effort to sell his book. It is scarcely necessary to say, that he did not take advantage of this singular concession. It was the 28th of February. A

* Manuscript Report of the Examination.

few days afterwards he did not require their permission. It was upon the proceeds of this reprint, and upon the humble legacy of Ernesta Viezzoli, that the Dictator and his family lived during the dictatorship.

CHAPTER II.

The Castellani and the Nicollotti—News of the French
Revolution of February—Decree of the Judges—
The Prisoners Guarded by the Police—Spielberg in
Prospect—News of the Revolution at Vienna—
Manin and Tommaseo Released—Manin at the
Square of San Mark—The Venetian Deputies, the
Viceroy, and the Archdukes—The Civic Guard—
Venice Rises—Manin, the Civic Authorities, and
the Governor—The Night of the 21st of March—
Preparations—Manin at the Arsenal—Manin Pro-
claims the Republic—The Governor and the Com-
mander Capitulate—Manin's Address to the Venetians
—Establishment of the Republican Government.

THE aspect of the city became more gloomy
every day. There was no carnival in 1848.
Strangers vainly sought in the new and sedate
Venice any traces of the gay Venice of the
eighteenth century. The money usually appropriated to *fétes* was sent to the wounded at
Milan. The old and feeble Venetian aristocracy
did not, like the Milanese nobility, commence the

movement, but they were drawn into it. The "*gardes nobles*," young men of ancient family, whom Austria had tried to attach to itself, by titles and uniforms, sent in their resignations to Vienna. An incident occurred among the lower classes of a very different nature and importance.

From the earliest times, the people of Venice had been divided into two factions, the *Castellani* and the *Nicolotti*—who took their titles from the two extremities of the city, the *Castle* and the suburb of *San Nicolo*—local factions, which were animated with all the ardour of political factions, but without any distinctive principles. These the aristocratic government tolerated as an outlet for the popular passions.* It even regulated their rivalry by authorizing annual athletic contests between the two parties. These at first consisted in unarmed combats, in which they contended with their fists for the possession of some of the bridges. Subsequently their contests assumed the more pacific although not less daring form of those gymnastic feats called "human pyramids," which, under the name of the *Feats of Hercules*, have found their way

*· The Nicolotti elected their doge, who was the head fisherman.

from the squares of Venice to the circuses of
Paris.

Under the French dominion, these athletic games
fell into disuse; under the Austrians, they were
succeeded by occasional regattas, in which the
old rivalry often led to sanguinary collisions, in
spite of the police and municipal authorities.

In proportion as public spirit became roused,
the intelligent youth of Venice made constant
efforts to reconcile the two popular factions, and
unite them against the common enemy—
Austria. Hitherto these efforts had been in
vain. *Nicolotti* and *Castellani* both maintained
that their honour was staked in the old quarrel.
" We can hate the Germans well enough," they
said, " without renouncing our faction."

The imprisonment of Manin and Tommaseo
turned their hearts. One morning, a number
of boats stopped before the steps of the church
of *Madonna della Salute*. The men who dis-
embarked wore, some the red scarfs of the
Castellani, others the black scarfs of the *Nicolotti*. Some were without any insignia—
the latter were the mediators. They entered
beneath the dome of the church, where a priest

awaited them.   He celebrated mass.   The two
chiefs of the reds and the blacks interlaced their
scarfs upon the steps of the altar, then served
as acolytes to the priest.   At the moment of
the elevation of the host, they, kneeling, raised
their right hands toward it.   They, and all
who were present, uttered in their hearts the
oath their lips were forbidden to pronounce.
This was, never again to fight, except against
the enemy of their country.   After the benediction, the two chiefs exchanged scarfs, and the
same day a banquet united the most ardent of
the late leaders of the two factions, wearing in-
discriminately red and black favours, with the
citizens who had effected their reconciliation.

Amid this crowded assembly of the lower
classes, sailors, fishermen, boatmen, butchers,
men of the humblest positions in society, not
an indiscretion was committed—not a sign escaped them which could lead the Austrian police
to suspect the political object of this reeonci-
liation.   Since that hour—in glory, as well as in
misfortune, not an infraction of the vow has
been committed.   The people kept and still
keeps its oath.

Soon afterwards a second *fête* day gave another diversion to the dulness of Venice. On the 6th February, news arrived that the revolution was successful in Sicily, and that Naples had imposed a constitution on King Ferdinand. The whole of Venetian society repaired, splendidly attired, to the theatre *Fenice;* the three Italian colours decorated, as if by magic, the boxes, stage, and performers, amid cries of, "Down with Austria!"

Meanwhile, the fate of the prisoners was revolving elsewhere than at Venice. From the 29th of January to the 17th of February, their examination was interrupted, and the depositions of the two captives were sent to the criminal tribunal of Milan, in the hope of obtaining a trial for high treason, which should include the principal leaders of the Lombardo-Venetian movement. Their heads were at stake. But, through the prudence, firmness, and patriotic unanimity of the witnesses examined at Venice against Manin and Tommaseo, this project failed. The tribunal of Milan could find no case against the chief of the conspiracy.

The tribunals hesitated. The government

redoubled its violence, and the people their excitement and animosity. Elsewhere, the Italian revolution made fresh progress every day. The King of Sardinia and the Grand Duke of Tuscany granted their subjects liberal constitutions (8—17 February), and the proclamation of the constitution by the pontiff at Rome, was impatiently expected day by day, for he was still the idol of the people of Italy. The incompatibility between legal liberty and a royalty associated with pontifical infallibility was not yet understood. The Austrians responded to the popular demonstrations by massacring the students of Pavia and Padua ;* and by the publication of an imperial rescript decreeing the penalty of death against every rebellion or provocation to rebel, " even if it were not followed by actual rebellion." (22nd February.)

The examination of Manin was resumed on the 17th of February. He did not change his plan of defence. The increasing menacing position of the country was imputed to him as a

---

* At Padua, on the day succeeding these butcheries, an Austrian soldier was seen on guard with pieces of human flesh sticking to his bayonet.

crime. He made it his defence—" A year ago,
a few reforms would have sufficed to have
blessed Austria; now nothing less than what I
have asked will suffice; but I do not know
whether what I have demanded will satisfy us
to-morrow." On the 28th of February, he
concluded by an earnest protest against the illegality of his detention, which was justified
neither by the legal proofs nor by his examination. Next day, great and exciting news reached
Milan and Venice. The government of July,
falling not so much by the errors of its home
policy, which might have been repaired, as
by its foreign policy, which had neither
satisfied the expectations, raised the grandeur,
nor employed the activity of France, gave way
before a question of reform, the solution of
which might have been quite pacific. A sudden
tempest had carried the Republic to the *Hotel
de Ville*. The position foreseen by Manin had
arrived. The revolution in France had rendered
Italian insurrection against Austria possible.
The keen glance of the statesman hesitated not
a moment as to the necessity for an active co-
operation between France and Italy—a necessity
which was so fatally disowned to the mutual

disaster of both nations! French newspapers
had reached Manin in his prison: he copied
with his own hand from the *National*, quoting
the *Journal des Debats :* "The Italians . . . .
will permit their French friends to share their
dangers, and pay to Italy a debt of gratitude for all
the blood Italians have shed in the French ranks."

The chances of Italy were increased tenfold;
but the personal danger of the captive was aggravated by the terrors of his persecutors.   On
the 5th of March, upon the decision of the
upright examining judge Zennari, the tribunal
of the first instance, composed of a majority of
Italians, declared that there was no legal charge
against Manin and Tommaseo: but the accused, having been arrested by the police, and
not by process of law, the tribunal was
obliged to remit them into the hands of the
police, which had arrested and still detained
them.   The danger of seeing the decision of
discharge reversed by the tribunals of Venice
and Verona, was among the least that assailed
the prisoners.   Everyone was aware that Governor Palffy had written to Vienna to request
the removal of Manin and Tommaseo to

Austria. Spielberg loomed in the distance ; the glorious future of Manin might be stifled at its birth. Nevertheless, the feeling of personal danger to the captive disappeared before the anxieties of the father. The consolation of being visited by his family was denied to him. His daughter's malady had become much worse, and the thought that this child, in her agony, should call in vain for him from her pillow, was to the father the cruelest of tortures.

But the patriot was not absorbed in the father. He had that within him which would suffice for every duty as well as suffering. From the depths of his dungeon his eye questioned alternately France and Germany, where resounded the menacing echoes of the 24th of February. The authorities no longer dared to conceal the official documents of France. The *Venice Gazette* of the 13th of March reprinted the eloquent manifesto drawn up by M. de Lamartine, in the name of the Provisional Government ; a manifesto which defended the Independent States of Italy against Austria, and which gave to the provinces occupied by the foreigner, if not positive assurance, at least encouraging

hopes.*   Two days later, news, much more
direct and immediate, spread over Venice, and
even penetrated Manin's prison.   Vienna was
in revolution!   The two most favourable conditions dreamed of by Manin were realised at
once, in France and in Germany.

From this moment Manin had no doubts
either of his approaching deliverance by the
hands of the people, nor of the imminence of
the *Lombardo-Venetian Vespers*.   "In the
silence of his prison he deeply meditated on the
future fate of his country, (and by *country*, he
understood not Venice only, but all Italy,) and
upon the course which Venice should take on
the desired day of deliverance, in order to place
her in harmony with the general progress of
Italy and with the French Revolution.   In an
hour I may be free, and my liberty will be the
freedom of Venice!   What must be done to
prevent anarchy from gliding in during the inevitable interval between the expulsion of the
Austrians and the constitution of Italian unity?

* "If in the decrees of Providence ...... the hour
of the reorganization of certain oppressed nationalities
appears to us to have arrived."

—Proclaim a constitutional king? That would only be a transition to a republic. Better go to the aim at once than to have a second revolution in prospect. Besides, the term 'constitutional king' would have no meaning for the people of Venice; they would not understand it. All our traditions, all our glory, is attached to the word Republic. Raise, then, the torch at which all the people of Italy will come one after another to light their liberties!"*

His course was decided; he awaited events with a resolute heart.

Day by day the popular demonstrations became more and more ardent. A decisive demonstration was resolved upon for the evening of the 16th. The people betook themselves to the *Fenice* theatre to demand the liberty of Manin and Tommaseo. The police, forewarned, closed the theatre. Next morning, the 17th of March, the people hastened, in feverish expectation, to watch the arrival of the Trieste packet, bringing news from Vienna. A French mer-

* We translate, almost literally, from the notes written by Signora Manin from the dictation of her husband, dated 17th of April, 1848.

chant, standing on the bridge of the steamer, shouted to the Venetian gondoliers—" Constitution at Vienna! Recognition of Italian Independence! Free press! National Guard!" *

The people rushed to the Governor's palace, and their improvised delegates demanded of Count Palffy the immediate release of the captives. The Governor sent the delegates to the judicial authorities. The President of the Court of Appeal sent them back to the Governor. The more excitable portion of the people lost patience, and hurried to the prison, the boys, as usual, at their head, among whom was the young son of Manin. The prison gates soon yielded to the impetuous attacks of these youths.

Meanwhile, Manin, his feelings soothed by a letter which announced some amelioration in the health of his daughter, was occupied in calculating (according to the *Augsburg Gazette*) the probable course the revolution would take in Germany,† when a loud uproar from the bridges

* Ricordi di Degli Antoni. MS.

† A de La Forge, v. i. p. 233. See the dramatic narrative of M. de La Forge, on the day of the 17th of March.

and quays attracted him to his window. He
was instantly recognized, and saluted with the
general cry of " *Viva Manin !*" The noise
at the entrance to the prison led him to suppose
that the gates were broken in. To him this
was an agonizing moment. Manin was sure
that his son was there, foremost in peril. He
saw the door of his cell open, the gaoler had
not troubled himself to shut it. Amid the
confusion into which the gaolers were thrown,
the prisoner happened to open a passage for
himself in order to meet his son. But Manin
stopped, it was not in this manner that he intended to go. Suddenly the chief gaoler came
in.

" Dress yourself quickly," he said, " and
come—you are free !"

" No !" replied Manin, " I wish to go by law,
and not by tumult; I have been arrested and
detained illegally. I wish to be released legally."

" But you are released by order of the Court."

" That makes a difference; I am at your
service."

Manin and Tommaseo met and embraced in

the corridor. At the bottom of the staircase they encountered the members of the tribunal in a body.

"Mr. President," said Manin, "I am not going out without a formal permission."

"The order is here," was the reply.

In fact, the Governor had given way, under the double pressure of news from Vienna and the Venetian revolt, and authorized the supreme court to act, that is, to enforce the law which the violence of the police had hitherto prevented from being carried into effect. Manin had attained his chief object—that of compelling the foreign authority to confess that it violated its own laws, and that it acted only in an arbitrary manner.

The people carried off the captives in triumph. Tommaseo, enfeebled by his imprisonment, upon reaching the open air fainted under the excitement of this glorious hour.

Manin, raised in a chair, as on a throne, was carried to the Square of St. Mark; that Venetian forum, where the people had so many times assembled to speak of their captivity and deliverance. The immense procession stopped under the balcony of the governor's residence. Count Palffy appeared on the balcony.

" Speak! speak !" cried voices on all sides to Manin.

" Speak ? What can I say ? Where are we ? I know nothing of what has happened !"

 " Constitution at Vienna ! Authority sent to the governor to release you !"

Manin then spoke as follows :—

" I am ignorant of the events by which I find myself released from the silence of a prison to be carried in triumph to the Square of St. Mark. But I judge from your faces and gestures that the sentiments of nationality and patriotism have made great progress during my captivity. I heartily rejoice at it, and thank you in the name of our country ; but forget not, I beg, that true and lasting liberty cannot exist without order, and you must make yourselves the emulous guardians of liberty to prove yourselves worthy of it."

The governor clapped his hands approvingly.

Manin continued :—

" Still, there are times and circumstances

when insurrection becomes not only a right but
a duty."

At hearing this the governor violently shut
his window. The people applauded vehemently.
Then the triumphal procession was resumed,
taking the direction of Manin's humble residence, in an obscure corner of an islet of San
Luca, where he had so often meditated and
watched for the day of deliverance which at
last had dawned. The crowd stopped at the
foot of the old tower of San Paternian, and
deposited the captive in the arms of his wife
and his dearly-loved daughter, who seemed restored to life by his return.

A thousand voices rent the air with this im-
promptu chorus :—

> " Viva Italia ! viva la liberta !
>   Viva Manin e Dio chi lo manda !"

" You must not praise me," cried Manin to
the people, " but him, who is the leader of the
Italian resurrection—Pius the Ninth !"

The Venetian patriot wished that the idea of
Italian unity should not cease for a moment
to predominate over Venice, and to the mass of

the people, this idea seemed personified in the still popular pontiff.

Paris and Vienna had changed everything. The first words of Manin on entering his house were—" The hour of deliverance has struck : we must act." He immediately conceived new plans for the new condition of things; but boldness demanded prudence. If the people rushed forward without arms or organization, they stood between the double peril of anarchy and a defeat that might restore the shattered tyranny. Already the Italian tricolour floated from the masts on the Square of St. Mark. A battalion of Croats advanced to tear down this ensign of revolution ; blood flowed ; the people, scattered by the bayonet, ran through the streets, crying " *Ai copi !*" (to the tiles !) Some young men rushed to Manin's house, and wished to bring him forth to head them. " This is not the way," said he, " we must form a civic guard."* And he sent one of his family to the governor. " Tell him," said he, " that to-day his life was in my hands, and that I

* Manuscript Notes of Signora Manin.

preached order, not vengeance ; and now, in the
interest of his life and of order, he must immediately organize a civic guard."*

The governor refused; but on the tumult
being renewed next morning, he authorized a
deputy of the Provincial Congregation to go and
confer with Manin. Manin and his friends replied by sending delegates to Count Palffy who
imperatively renewed the demand of the city.
The governor urged that he had no authority,
and sent the delegates to the viceroy. Two of
the delegates immediately set out for Milan.
They did not reach it, for at Verona they encountered the viceroy, the Archduke Regnier,
who had quitted Milan to avoid imminent dangers, leaving the responsibility in the hands of
Radetsky.

The deputies found the Lombardo-Venetian
kingdom disorganized, the viceroy timid, helpless, and terrified, very anxious to know, during

---

* Previous to the revolution, he had announced it
to those who came to congratulate him upon his deliverance, and they were all unanimous on the impossibility of obtaining any such concession from Austria.—
Ricordi di Degli Antoni.

the exciting events around him, if he could go
as usual and take his salt-water baths at Venice !
his young sons, exasperated and furious, declaim-
ing in terms that cannot be repeated against that
government of women which at Vienna did not
at the onset shoot down the Viennese not dreaming only of blood and carnage.* The civil and

* "She (the vice-queen) asked me if I would have
been pleased to see the troops come to blows and blood-
shed ? I could only reply 'Yes.' They say that they
fired on the people in the square of St. Mark, and that ;
five men were killed. 'There is no great harm in that
if anything takes place at Milan, I hope for the Milanese
that at least five hundred will be left dead on the
square.'"—(Letter from the Archduke Regnier, son of
the viceroy, dated 19th March.) Next day, on the news
of the struggle at Milan, "At the Broletto some twelve-
pounders would have made fine work of it ; they ought
to shoot all the prisoners ; martial law should be declared ; it is the only way... If, indeed, a good many
had been left dead on the square—the soldiers would have
shown but little moderation in an assault."—(Letter of
the 20th March.) We do not repeat what was said respecting the imperial family at Vienna ; at the same time
we may remark that the *petticoat government* neglected
nothing to regain the esteem of the young archduke, and
the doing of Hungary ought at least to have satisfied
him. The letters above quoted, intercepted by the

military councillors were divided : the people at
Verona, as everywhere else, rising *en masse*
under the Italian tricolour.

On the 19th of March the viceroy, after
much hesitation, granted permission to arm
four hundred citizens at Verona and two hundred
at Venice. Venice did not wait for this mocking
concession to arm itself. The previous evening, upon hearing that the governor had sent
the deputies to the viceroy, Manin declared
to his friends that there was no time for
waiting, that the civic guard must be formed
immediately, and putting himself at their head,
he presented to the municipal authorities, for
signature, a petition to the governor, already
prepared in the name of this body. He

Italians, were inserted, with some suppressions, due to
Venetian courtesy, in the first volume of a collection
published at Venice during the revolution, at intervals,
according to circumstances. (*Raccolta per ordine cro-
nologico di tutti gli atti, decreti, etc.; del governo prov-
visorio di Venezia, non che scritti, avvisi etc. di citta-
dini, privati, etc.* vols. viii. in 8vo.) The Austrians
vainly endeavoured to suppress this precious collection,
which is one of the principal sources of our narrative.

concluded his address to the municipal body
with these energetic words:

"We have defended liberty with words, we
shall now defend it with bullets."

The mayor and his associates signed the petition, and proceeded in a body to the governor.
As they were departing, Manin said to them,
"If you obtain the authority, so much the
better; if you do not obtain it, we will do without it." And, together with his friends, he set
himself to work to draw up the rules and regulations for the civic guard. Meanwhile the
whole city had risen; the bridges were barri-
caded, every roof covered with people, armed
with tiles. The fight between the people and
the Croatian infantry was renewed more violently than on the previous evening, on the
square of St. Mark; the fusillade resounded
through the city—the people, as before, ran for
Manin, and he had again the courage to refuse
them: a general occupied in arranging his plans
of battle does not quit his tent to risk his life
at the outposts.

During this interval, the reply of the governor to the municipal body was received. It

was still in the negative. "Now, then, is the time!" said Manin; "let every one go home and arm himself!" And he ran to San Pater-nian, called his son, and set out with him, gun in hand, and in half an hour he was at the head of the nucleus of a civic guard of citizens and workmen. His first address to his troop is characteristic.

"Let those only who will implicitly obey me remain with me." They all remained.

The crisis was modified from this very mo-ment. The reiterated application of the muni-cipal officers and of the patriarch, and especially the uncertainty of success if the combat became serious, had induced the governor to yield. He consented to the organizing of two hundred men as a civic guard, who were to receive their orders from the directors of public safety; that is to say, *from the police.**

Manin troubled himself very little about the conditions. He returned to the municipal pa-lace, calming the people on his way, sending the artizans to their workshops, with the pro-

* *Ricordi di Degli Antoni.* M. A. de La Forge says four hundred.

mise to send for them when wanted, and ordered
the shops to be reopened.   Workmen and shop-
keepers listened with an intelligent docility, and
in entire confidence.   He proceeded to the city-
hall, and found there the deputy chief of the
police, a German, who had come to superintend
the drawing up of the regulations of the new
institution.   When he saw that instead of two
hundred, there were already more than two
thousand on the muster roll, while the roll was
still left open for more, the Austrian exclaimed—

" You are getting up a revolt, then; do you
want to compel me to put the city in a state of
siege ?"

" I am here," replied Manin, " to restore
order ; but if you put any obstacle in the way
of the measures necessary to maintain it"—
(and he rose up impetuously, seizing his gun)—
" I will call to arms the people I have appeased,
and will put myself at the head of the insurrection."*

The police officer retired.   The governor,
through one of his agents, endeavoured to persuade the municipality to disavow Manin's act,

* *Ricordi di Degli Antoni.*

and to issue a proclamation reminding the people
that the *judicio statuario* (the imperial rescript
decreeing the penalty of death in every case of
rebellion) was still in force.   Manin repeated his
menaces.   The negociator urged, " Suppose,
which is impossible, that you drive us out of the
city, could you keep it four-and-twenty hours ?"
"Place the city in my hands," replied Manin,
" I shall know how to defend it."*

The governor learned at the same time the
refusal of the municipality, and the news from
Vienna of the imperial government having confirmed and extended its promises to the Viennese revolution.   He resigned himself to following the example, made an attempt at being popular, read the dispatch from Vienna to the people
from his balcony, and declared that he had
asked the emperor to grant radical reforms, and
that he should rejoice to become the first constitutional governor of Venice.

Venice was illuminated at night, and Manin's

* A. de La Forge, v. i. p. 247, 248. The apparent
contradiction between De La Forge and Degli Antoni is
due to the fact that there were two successive scenes at
the city hall, and each describes but one.

guard patrolled the city amid the blessings of
the people.

The first pass-word given to the civic guard
was *fratellanza* (fraternity).   Venice continued
faithful.

Next morning, the 19th March, the Venetian
Official Gazette applauded, in the name of the
governor, the revolution of Vienna.   In the
first moments of enthusiasm the good-natured
Italians had *vivas* for everybody, even for Count
Palffy.   Manin alone remained calm and unmoved.   He knew the value of *Austrian faith;*
he knew that it was necessary they should be
on their guard against surprises, against trickery.
Notice of sinister designs, of projects of bombardment, were soon communicated to him by workmen in the arsenal, and by a naval officer.

Again, were the Austrians sincere? where
would they be if the revolution was stopped?
Venice and Lombardy, members of the *Constitutional* Empire of Austria!   Before the 24th
of February, this was a position to which Manin
appeared to resign himself for his country,*

* We say *appeared*, as he asked, but did not reckon
upon obtaining it.

but matters had ripened quickly; instead of reform, revolution had come; now he must rush past the halting-place, and go straight to the goal—NATIONAL INDEPENDENCE ! EXPULSION OF THE FOREIGNER ! *

Manin had an organized force in hand—he must use it. The opportunity had come; the garrison was small; only a single Croatian regiment was true; two Italian regiments sympathised with the people; the enemy must not have time to strengthen itself. Manin had no other idea than to fight; he shrugged his shoulders when urged to endeavour to constitute the government of Venice in face of the foreigner's cannon still in position on the public squares. To govern the city, he must possess the city. The municipality, on account of the gravity of the circumstances, had enlisted many eminent citizens into its body. Manin declined to take part in the *aggiunta*—he wished to have his hands free; the *advocate* had disappeared; the

---

* In any case it was too late to stop. It was not known to Manin that at this very hour the streets of Milan ran with its citizens' blood. War to the knife had commenced.

tribune, and soon the dictator, rose up. The man of law was now the man of revolution.

Three days elapsed; during which the revolution, like the revolt, proceeded orderly. The civic guard armed and disciplined itself, and increased until it now reckoned no less than four thousand men. They took the military positions in the interior, one after another, or shared them with the troops of the line. The first day, the 18th of March, Manin sent to the 1st civic guard an inoffensive white scarf;* the commander of the city having declared that the tricoloured cockade would be treated as the ensign of sedition. The 20th of March, Manin, with the green, red, and white cockade, defiled, with his company, before the Austrian post, in the square of St. Mark. The guard presented arms to him. On the 21st, Count Palffy demanded a conference with him. "Tell the governor," replied Manin to the envoy, "that he did not wish to hear me when he could grant what I wished; and as now, he cannot grant what I should demand if I

* It was afterwards retained as a sign of fraternity.

ask anything else of him, I should deceive him ; and I have never deceived anybody."

A young naval officer, a Venetian and patriot, like most of the corps, had already informed Manin of the preparations made for bombarding the city, and pressed him to attack the arsenal. On this 21st of March, he again warned Manin of these preparations. " To-morrow," said Manin, " the city will be in my power, or I shall be dead."

Meanwhile the same feelings and apprehensions excited an *émeute* among the workmen at the arsenals.

In the evening, at the city hall, Pincherle the merchant, a friend of Manin's, and one of the new members added to the municipality, repeated to the municipal corps a question which he had asked several times during the two preceding days—" If the Austrian dominion falls, will you have the strength and courage to take charge of the government ? "

This time the question was discussed : but the discussion only ended in charging Pincherle to go and ask Manin why he kept aloof from the municipality, and what his projects were.

Pincherle found Manin holding a conference with several of the most influential patriots : they were deliberating upon the future government of Venice, and upon the rallying cry they should give to the people.. Some had no hope of an Italian administration under the constitutional empire of Austria ; others wished to raise the cry of "*Viva Piedmont,*" and to strive for the union of Venice with the kingdom of Charles Albert. The majority, as a kind of medium course, proposed to cry, " *Viva Rainieri* (the Archduke Regnier), the constitutional king ;" and to demand the erection of the Lombardo-Venetian vice-royalty into a kingdom.

" Piedmont ?" said Manin, "you don't know yet if it will accept you.—The Vienna constitution?—King Rainieri?—No ! no ! You must have complete independence ! No half revolution, which will soon require you to make another No negotiations with Austria ! it would only be a loss of precious time. We can free our country only by force. We must seize the arsenal first thing. If I have called you together, it is in order to plan a popular movement for to-morrow, sustained by the civic guard. As for the government, the people of Venice can only comprehend one cry, " *Viva la Repubblica !*"

But they all hesitated; not from want of sympathy, but from want of faith. On the previous evening, one of the best and greatest, a noble heart, replied to Manin's expression of confidence only by a sad smile. " The people are incapable of sacrifices !" " You do not know them," cried Manin : " I know them, and that is my sole merit. You'll see !" *

Pincherle was introduced. Manin directed him to go and say to the municipality, that he could not communicate his plans to the whole municipal body, but he would confide them to the mayor, if he would come to him next morning at seven o'clock. He also begged Pincherle

---

* This anecdote is in A. de La Forge, v. i. p. 257—258. All the details of what transpired during the night of the 21st—22nd of March, with Manin and the municipality, are taken from the MS. account of Degli Antoni, and from notes written a few days subsequent to the events, by Signora Teresa Manin and her daughter Emilia. That which refers to Piedmont, is found in the notes of Emilia Manin. .

to draw aside the advocate Avesani, one of the additional members, a clever, decisive man, and bring him back the same night. When Pincherle returned late at night with Avesani, Manin was alone, exhausted by the efforts he had made to convince his friends. The meeting had separated, without coming to any conclusion.* Manin roused himself to persuade the new-comers. "We must have the Republic," he said; "and to the cry of *Viva la Repubblica,* we must add another, *Viva San Marco!* that will find an echo in Dalmatia."†

"*Viva San Marco!* the old Venetian cry! You are right: it is the people's rallying cry, and the only one possible!"

Like the cities of antiquity, Venice had, in fact, from its origin, its local genius, a personification of country: and this genius was the apostle of the winged lion. Manin shook his guests by the hand. "We are agreed then;"

---

* *Ricordi di Degli Antoni.* According to De La Forge, the meeting would have concluded in favour of King Rainieri. It is probable that the majority, at least, remained of that feeling.

† *Ricordi di Degli Antoni,* p. 6.

and he retired to meditate during the few hours that intervened before action. Some devoted friends guarded his door, to protect him from an increasing host of advisers. About six in the morning, an unknown, who could not force his way past the guard, declared to the friend charged by Manin with receiving the bearers of advice, that he was the Sardinian Consul Faccanoni ; and that he came to advise the Venetians to raise the cry of *"Viva la Repub- blica! Viva Manin, President!"* and he boldly proclaimed his advice.*

At the same moment, Manin, who had only assumed the rank of captain in the civic guard, sent for Mengaldo, the Commander-in-Chief of this guard. " The city is threatened with bom- bardment," he said. " I wish, at any risk, to take the arsenal. You must make me Com- mander-in-Chief for a day. Form the six batta- lions into two brigades, and place the captains at my disposal for eight hours."

The general, overcome by the authoritative

---

* See the relation by Casarini, in the documents given in De la Forge, v. i. p. 347.

manner of the audacious advocate, withdrew
without replying.

Next moment Count Correr, the mayor,
arrived. Manin declared plainly to him, that
he was going, that very morning, to drive the
Austrians out of Venice. "Now you know my
reason for not going to the city hall : this is not
a subject upon which we could deliberate in
council."

Mengaldo returned. He had reflected upon
Manin's demand. He was a brave man, and a
good patriot ; but an old officer of the empire,
and, like all military men, with no confidence in
irregular forces, or in the efforts of the masses.

"Before giving the lives of thousands of my
fellow-citizens into your hands, I must know
what you propose to do with them."

"I don't know yet; I only know that I shall
succeed."

"That is madness. I cannot join you."* And
he retired. This was a serious matter : everything
might be compromised and baffled by this refusal. Manin went and demanded the company
of which he was captain. The adjutant-major

* A. de la Forge, t. i. p. 262.

—the advocate Benvenuti, refused it to him. Of the whole company, his son alone stood by him. He then despatched Degli Antoni to all the chiefs of the city guard, upon whom he believed he could rely, and requested them to assemble with their men at noon; some on the square of St. Mark, the others in the vicinity of the arsenal. At ten o'clock, the young naval officer, Salvani, who had been many times before to Manin, now came, exclaiming,—"To the arsenal! to the arsenal! now, or never! The marines are on our side! Be quick; or Venice will be bombarded and sacked!"

Degli Antoni returned. Manin sent him a second time, to entreat Benvenuti to give him a few resolute, well-armed men. "I shall not place my men at the mercy of a madman," was Benvenuti's reply. Manin really despaired for a moment. To have brought everything so happily to the decisive hour, and to see the deliverance of his country torn from his hands by his own friends, even! "I have done my duty," he cried: "the fault will not be mine!"*

* *Ricordi di Degli Antoni :* notes of Madame Manin and her daughter.

If he could not free the city, he wished, at least, to save it. He dictated to Degli Antoni notes to the principal consuls, entreating them, in the name of humanity, and for the safety of their countrymen, to protest against the bombardment.*

It was now half-past eleven. Olivo, the chief of the battalion of the *quartier* San Polo, arrived. He had responded to Manin's appeal. A ray of joy reappeared in Manin's eyes. " At noon come, everyone, to the square of St. Mark." During this interval, sad news was brought. Colonel Marinovich, second in command of the arsenal, and the presumed agent of the plan of bombardment, had been massacred by a band of workmen in the arsenal. Manin's anticipations were realised. Anarchy prevailed. A reaction would take place immediately without doubt ! The enemy had now a pretext for revenge ! Not a moment to lose !

Embracing his daughter, and drawing his wife apart, he recommended her not to lose heart if a few bombs fell upon the city. Then

* See the correspondence of Manin with the British consul, in A. de la Forge. Vol. i. pp. 264, 348, 349.

calling to his son George, he exclaimed—" To the arsenal."

" Who knows whether you will return to-night ?" said his wife to him jestingly, in presence of their daughter. She smiled, but her heart was full of anguish. She received no reply.

They set forth, the father with sword in hand, the son with gun upon his shoulder. Two friends remained to protect the wife and daughter : they had sworn to die on the threshold.

Manin enlisted some civic guards, one by one, on his way : he arrived at the square of Saint Mark : Olivo and his men were not there. Degli Antoni rejoined Manin, bringing with him the reply of the British consul, who could see no signs of a bombardment being imminent : to his written reply,* the consul had added verbally, his advice to the Venetians to keep themselves quiet : he said, he could not prevent the government from taking the measures it deemed necessary to restore order.†

* Letter from Emilia Manin, of the 26th of March.
† *Ricordi di Degli Antoni.*

Manin tore up this letter indignantly. " Forward," said he. The little troop gradually increased. It soon numbered one hundred men, most of them with no other arms than their swords. He divided them into two sections, to give them the appearance of peaceful patrols. They soon appeared before the naval arsenal.

He found two chiefs of battalion, and a group of civic guards, at the gate : and in the confusion that followed upon the murder of Colonel Marinovitch, about a dozen of these guards were allowed to pass in. Manin also passed in. He directed Degli Antoni to introduce all the civic guards who were present, a few at a time, as well as others that might come. He then had an interview with Martini, commander of the marines, and boldly demanded that the arsenal should be surrendered to the civic guard. Martini exclaimed against it, protested that the projects of violence imputed to the government were unfounded, and authorised the citizens then present to satisfy themselves that no preparations for bombardment existed in the arsenal. While three of the citizens proceeded with the search, Manin demanded that several gun-boats in the lagoon, on which Croats with lighted matches were stationed, should be disarmed. The three citizens who returned from the inspection, announced that the Croatian infantry, which occupied the land arsenal, could carry the naval arsenal by merely knocking down a wooden railing.

"You must give me your cannon," said Manin to Martini.

"Never," was the reply.

"But it is done," said a naval officer; "I have given them up to the civic guard."

"Your ammunition, then!" resumed Manin.

The commander acceded. Manin immediately proceeded to turn the guns on the Croats, and in conjunction with the naval officers, made suitable arrangements for order and defence.*

Upon his return, he found the commander, who had attempted to go away, detained prisoner by the civic guard. He ordered the bell to be rung to summon the workmen to the arsenal, who had been dismissed after the death of

* "The command of the arsenal will be given to Praziani, that of the fleet to Marsich, that of the artillery and marines to Paolucci."—*Ricordi di Degli Antoni.*

Marinovitch, and demanded the keys of the armoury. Martini's people pretended they could not be found. " If the keys are not given to me in five minutes," said Manin, " I shall break open the doors." The keys were soon brought.

Manin then armed the civic guards and the workmen—organised the latter into companies, and distributed the command. Hereupon a touching scene ensued. An old officer, Colonel Graziani, appointed commander of the naval arsenal in place of Martini, struggling between devotion to his country, and duty to his flag, fell upon his knees, and, with tears in his eyes, implored Martini to release him from his oath. Martini refused. Graziani felt that there existed natural and inviolable duties, against which the arbitrary conventions of man ought not to prevail. He decided.* The cry " To arms" was raised. A column of marines placed themselves before the gate of the arsenal. The civic guard made preparations for defence. Major Broday, commander of the infantry, ordered them to

* Ricordi di Degli Antoni.   † Idem.
‡ Notes of Madame Manin.

fire.   The soldiers grounded their arms : they
were Italians.   One of them made a thrust
with his bayonet at the Major; the people
rushed upon him.   He was rescued and saved
by Degli Antoni, and kept prisoner.

The work of the arsenal was finished. Manin
went out, and on passing through the gate, cried
*Viva la Republica ! Viva l'Italia ! Viva Pio
Nono ! Viva San Marco !*

The old Venetian cry, after fifty years' silence,
again awoke the echoes of the lagoons.

"*Viva la Republica !*" cried Manin, which
was responded to by long and unanimous acclamations.

"To the square of St. Mark," said Manin to
those around him.   "You go and spread yourselves all over the city, and call the people to
Saint Mark's."

Then he entered a tavern with his son and
two friends, in order to take a little repose, and
allow time for the people to respond to his
summons.   It was now three o'clock.   At four
he re-appeared, proclaimed "their saviour" by
all the people on that same square of St. Mark,
which at noon he had crossed with his son in

expectation of meeting certain death. He mounted a table, from which, soaring above the sea of heads that covered the forum of Venice, with sword in one hand, and bearing in the other the Italian tri-coloured flag, he addressed the crowd :

" Venetians, we are free ! and we may doubly congratulate ourselves with being so, as it has been accomplished without the shedding of one drop of our blood, or of that of our brothers, for to me all men are brothers !—To have overturned the old government is not all : we must establish a new one : the best for us appears to me to be the Republic, which will recall past glory ; and then add the liberty of modern times to it. By this we shall not separate ourselves from our Italian brothers ; but, on the contrary, form one of those centres which will aid in the successive fusion of our Italy into one whole ! *Viva*, then, the Republic ! *Viva* liberty ! *Viva* Saint Mark !"*

Thunders of applause passed from isle to isle to the extremities of Venice. The civic guard formed itself into a hollow square, and with

* Notes of Emilia Manin.

drawn swords, swore to defend to the last drop
of its blood, the new Republic and its founder.

"Thus," wrote the amiable wife of Manin
some weeks afterwards, "Thus ended tyranny
in Venice, thus liberty revived; in this manner
was accomplished a revolution that overwhelmed
our contemporaries with stupefaction, and which
posterity will look upon as fabulous! Mortal
speech is too feeble to express the joy, the delirium in which the people are revelling. The
old weep, the young embrace; hands are fran-
tically clapped together, or raised in gratitude
to heaven."

An old man, on hearing the Republic proclaimed, drew from his bosom an old image of
a lion carved in wood: "I well knew that Venice
would rise again," he cried; "for fifty years
I have kept this lion to bring it forth on the
day it would be again republican! I have nothing
more to ask of Heaven. I can die happy
now!"*

An immense procession of the people reconducted the liberator in triumph, and deposited
him, overcome with joy and fatigue, with his

---

* Riminiscenze di A. Giustinan.

wife and daughter, who fainted upon seeing him. From the time he had left his prison, for five days and nights, Manin had scarcely closed his eyes, and was all this time a prey to suffering most incompatible with the physical activity demanded by the part he now played.

Ever since the 17th of March, he had thought, spoken, and acted without intermission. Tortured by an acute inflammation of the kidneys, and feeling the insidious attacks of a still more serious disorder, he sank exhausted, saying, "Leave me at least, this night, to rest, or I shall die."

He was aware that others had undertaken to conclude and regulate in some measure his revolutionary work. While he was occupied in taking the arsenal, the same general of the civic guard, Mengaldo, who had refused to co-operate in the attack, attempted to arrive at the same result pacifically, by inviting the governor to resign all the military positions into the hands of the civic authorities, or, in other words, to capitulate. Palffy demanded a conference with the municipal corps.* The municipality de-

* *Ricordi di Degli Antoni.*

spatched commissioners to the governor.   Avesani, their spokesman, distinguished himself by
his energy, and imperatively insisted upon the
evacuation.   This was a very bitter moment for
the great Count Palffy, who had been heard to say
that " there would be no use for cannon against
the Italians : a stick would do for them."   He
knew that the arsenal was taken.   The cries
from the Square of St. Mark, proclaiming Manin and the Republic, reached even the governor's palace.   Palffy resigned his powers, not
into the hands of the municipality, but into those
of the commander of the place, Field-Marshal-
Lieutenant Count Zichy.   The Hungarian Zichy
was an enlightened and humane man, and his
dearest, inmost feelings were for the Italians.
He well knew that he risked his head by not
acting defensively ; but to defend Venice against
its citizens would be a crime against civilization ;
for hostilities in this city, filled with treasures
of art, would be the cause of irreparable disasters ; and even if he ventured to fight he could
not win.   The Italian and half-Italian troops
had melted away in his hands like snow ; and it
was not with two battalions of Croats, and some

German artillery, less than twenty-five hundred
men in all,* that he could expect to reconquer
Venice. He signed a capitulation, which cost
him very dear ;† but history at least will render
him justice, and abjure the charges of weakness
and cowardice laid on his head.

The Austrian commander abdicated into the
hands of the provisional government, of which
the municipal commissioners assumed the responsibility. He pledged himself to evacuate
Venice with all his foreign mercenaries ; the
Italian troops, the material of war, and the public treasury to remain.

In the evening a proclamation from the provisional government officially announced the fall
of the Austrian government, and the terms that
had been concluded with it. The people were
astonished and irritated in not seeing on this
document the names of Manin and Tommaseo,
nor even that of the Republic. Degli Antoni
hastened to communicate this feeling to Manin.

* Letter from the English consul, Clinton Dawkins,
in A. de la Forge, vol. ii. p. 205.

† He was condemned to death. This sentence was
commuted to imprisonment for life.

"They have performed an act of mercy," cried Manin. "I have worked enough, but give them this piece of news." This was the adhesion given in advance to the Republic by the Sardinian consul.

"There is something else to do at this moment," replied Avesani to Degli Antoni, "besides discussing the form of government."

"They must do as they like!" said Manin, on receiving this response. "I wash my hands of it."

"How can you take things with such indifference?" asked Degli Antoni.

"Make yourself easy. You will see that they must have recourse to me."

Fearing the consequences of the popular discontent, he dictated the following proclamation from his bed :—

"VENETIANS!

"I know that you love me; and, in the name of that love, I ask you to conduct yourselves, during the legitimate manifestation of your joy, with that dignity which belongs to men worthy of being free.

"Your friend,

"MANIN."

His brother-in-law, Degli Antoni, immediately caused these noble words to be printed and placarded on every wall in Venice.

The people understood them. The first night of liberty was passed without the slightest disorder. Only the most notable members of the Venetian *bourgeoise* met together, and sent to the governmental commission to express its dissatisfaction at the exclusion of Manin, and to demand the dismissal of Avesani, the president of the Commission. The Commission resigned ts powers into the hands of one of its members, Mengaldo, Commander of the civic guard. This was at half-past three o'clock, on the morning of the 23d of March, too late by an hour ! For an error had been committed that night, as we shall see, the consequences of which could not be averted.*

* *Ricordi di Degli Antoni.* Many prejudices existed against Avesani, which we cannot enter into in this place. Avesani now endures his exile with a dignity which wins for him the respect of every one. It is quite certain, according to De la Forge, that Manin did not share these prejudices, and that he wished to associate Avesani in his government.

As Manin had predicted, he was sent for; for the revolution he had made would be governed only by him. In the morning, Mengaldo, the mayor Correr, and some other men of intelligence and experience, assembled at Manin's bed-side.   He took counsel with them, and then proceeded to the municipality, still crowded with the elite of the citizens.

Entering, less as a tribune than as a dictator, this time, he imposed rather than proposed, his plans and his list of ministers, with that kind of despotism peculiar to great men of action at decisive moments, and which, with him, was an absolute abnegation.   He loved not power for power's sake; he was not a man to encroach by strength or cunning; in a crisis, he admitted no half-confidence; he must be accepted or rejected wholly.   Among the members of his government he had placed Pincherle, a Jew, and an artisan, the tailor Toffoli, as pledges of religious liberty and political equality; both these men proved themselves worthy of representing two great principles.

At two o'clock the civic guard was summoned to meet at the square of St. Mark; the religious

head of Venetia, the patriarch, who followed
the movement after first holding himself aloof
from it, blessed the tricoloured flag in the name
of Pius the Ninth.   The Italian flag exchanged
a fraternal salute with the flags of the French and
American Republics.   Then the commander,
Mengaldo, proposed the list of the ministry to
the civic guard and to the people.   The list was
accepted with shouts of " *Viva Manin!* President of the Republic!" and this devoted people
united in its acclamations the names of its mar-
tyrs, the brothers Bandiera and Moro, with that
of its liberator.*   The Venetian government

* We find in the notes of Emilia Manin a page
which, amid the narratives of this happy day, resembles
a knell sounding sadly among festal chimes.   The poor
child, analysing her feelings with a singular vigour of
thought and expression, expresses remorse at not being
" filled with an ineffable joy " when she found herself,
for the first time after his deliverance, under the majestic
arches of St. Mark, in presence of her father, proclaimed
liberator of his country.   " I ought to be at the summit
of happiness, but a weight continually oppresses my
heart."   This burden never left her for a moment except when she saw the battalions of the civic guard
called into existence by her father, defile past in imposing array.   All the emotions of the daughter found

was reconstituted ; a new phase in the life of
Manin commenced.

their echo in the heart of her father. Manin never
passed a day of unmingled happiness.

We place in connection with the daughter's notes a
letter written by her mother, which, although different
in sentiment, is not inferior in character.

TERESA MANIN TO MADAM C———.

Venice, 3rd April, 1848.

DEAR FRIEND,

The delirium in which we have lived for some
days past, and from which we have not yet escaped, has
not permitted me to occupy myself with anything, and
this has delayed my replying to you. Everything, even
my own family, of which I generally take such care, has
been neglected. Thinking of the marvellous events
which have delivered us from a tyranny of thirty-three
years has been my only occupation. These events are
like a dream ; our present position is like a vision. Oh !
dear friend, understand our felicity ! To rise from our
bed *slaves*, and return to it at night *free !* If that does
not seem like a dream, what can be so ? Dear friend,
why are you not here on this day of our redemption ?
Such days never occur twice in the course of one human
existence.

I suffered much before this day of recompense arrived, for I knew perfectly well to what dangers my
husband exposed himself. But I never said to him—
Stop ! And yet, I assure you, seeing him almost beside

himself from the great pressure on his mind in meditating on the form of government it would be advisable to adopt, I have sometimes trembled for his reason.

But my anxiety and terror were greatest when he informed me that Venice might possibly be bombarded that day . . . . . When I saw him write to the different consuls to protest against this measure, and when I heard him call George, and say to him, "Come with me to the arsenal!" what I suffered at that moment you can imagine much better than I can describe. I think few women would have conducted themselves as I did. I embraced neither my husband nor my son, so that I should not delay them. What hours were those, from one till five! I felt sure that if either of my beloved were killed, the other would certainly share his fate.

At last, at about five o'clock, the shouts of a great crowd approaching our house delivered my heart from its anguish. I distinctly heard cries of *Viva Manin!* From this moment I felt sure of success. *Viva San Marco! Viva la Republica!* I cried in my turn, for I was sure that my husband would not return until he had proclaimed the Republic in the Square of St. Mark.

For the second time in five days I saw my husband brought in triumph to his house. Twice in five days! that was too much for my nerves! Still I sustained myself in my joy as I had done in my grief. I embraced my husband as the liberator, the chief among all, of my country. I embraced my son, who, at the age of sixteen, had displayed the courage and coolness of mature years. . . . . And I was proud of both.

I have a thousand things to say, but have not time. I read your letter, and that of citizen Louis, to my husband, and he was greatly moved.   For your son also, he bids me tell you, a great and glorious career is opened in our Republic.   Whoever combines honesty with talent, will find honour and recompense.   That is indisputable.   The future of your son is therefore assured, dear friend.   I must conclude.

.   .. Your TERESA.

CHAPTER III.

Manin's Policy—Revolt of Venetia—The affair of the
Squadron—Radetsky driven out of Milan—Revolt
of Lombardy—The Question of Appeal to France—
Manin, Tommaseo, and the French Provisional Go-
vernment — What ought France to do? —Charles
Albert, *Fara da sé*—The Milanese—The Republic of
Venice is not officially recognized at Paris—State of
the Austrian Army—Affair of the *Lloyd's*.

THE city was free ; but was the whole country
free ? Would Venice remain free by the deliverance of Italy ? Manin was not one of those
who become intoxicated by a first success. He
was not ignorant of the immense complexity of
the elements, amid which the Italian revolution
progressed. A success was possible ; that was
enough for him ; he believed it, and felt it his
duty to act. He was not sure of victory ; but

he was, at least, certain of elevating the honour
of his country.   He well understood the people
which Europe judged so harshly, and he thought
that Italy, once in action, might still be unfortunate, but never again despised.   He was sure,
at least, of his Venice, and knew what he
could do for her.   Oblige the world to think
better of Italy; show the world that, happen
what might, she was living and indestructible,
and at last obtain for her the respect of nations.
This idea, in which lay his true greatness, occupied his mind even more than his success.
" You call us talkers, mere theatrical declaimers,"
he wrote subsequently.   " I hope you will not
always be able to speak thus of Venice." *   And
he entered upon his career in this splendid city,
where everything partakes of show and splen-
dour, by showing the successor of the Doges
that he could govern with the simplicity of forms
of an American puritan.   " The days of artistic
Italy are past," he said, " let us see another
Italy !"

The good sense of the people understood this,
that the greatest prestige for it was to have no

* Manuscript notes.

prestige.* No appeal to the imagination, which over-excites, then leaves their hearts more feeble than before; not to dazzle the people, but to govern them by their judgment and their feeling; never to give way to injustice, and never seek a perilous auxiliary in the blind passions of the people. "The people (and the whole mass of men is the people!) has its generous as well as its ferocious instincts," observed Manin; "it is a misfortune if it be allowed to obey the latter; it then becomes savage. The first drop of blood spilt creates a thirst for blood, which can neither be diverted nor stopped. Hence the necessity for opposing such a tendency with desperate energy."†

A single murder, that of Marinovitch, had

* What displeased me in Italy, was the fault of declamation, of exaggeration. I prefer the opposite, perhaps to an extreme. I abstain as much as possible from pomp, display, or theatrical ceremonies; I always have a maxim of Tommaseo's in my mind, "The truly courageous soldier fights, and holds his tongue." Foreigners call us talkers. My desire is that they may not in future be able to say this of Venice.—(MS. Notes.) "To abstain from pomp is a sign that we are inclined to return to private life."—(Ibid.)

† Manuscript Notes.

stained the revolution of Venice with blood.*
Manin was decided, at the sacrifice of his life,
not to allow a second.

The principles from which he regarded himself
as bound never to depart were these—justice and
order within, inflexible firmness without.   No
negotiations with Austria to be entertained—the
attempts at peaceful reform had proved useful in
preparing the revolution—but the revolution once
come, all negociation would be but a snare—every
promise made by Austria would be infallibly violated.   Any arrangement which would recognise
the least right whatever in Austria over Italy,
would bring back foreign tyranny   Strict union
with the various Italian States, whatever their
form of government, provided they cooperated in
the war of independence, and until an Italian representative assembly had decided the organization of the Peninsula.   A particularly intimate
union with Lombardy, sister both in their bondage
and in their deliverance.   Appeal to the French
alliance, which followed of necessity from the
resolve never to make terms with Austria.

* Besides, the cause of this murder was more private and personal than political: the workmen detested
this officer for his severity.

All these views he had well considered in his mind previously.* Between the turmoils of government and the turmoils of war there was no more time for long meditations. Events followed each other like thunder-claps. The issue of the conflict which had lasted many days at Milan was still unknown; but that insurrection approached nearer and nearer was well understood. During the night of the 22nd and 23rd of March the civic guard of the village of Mestra carried the great fortress of Malghera, which commanded the railway of Venice. The energetic population of Chioggia made the citadel capitulate on the evening of the 23rd. All the suburbs of Venice, lagoon and shore, were taken, almost without a blow. On the 24th, Padua, which the division of General di Aspro had kept down, was hastily abandoned by this Austrian corps, which was bad news for

* The spirit of his government was manifested in his first acts. On the 23rd of March, a decree, promising complete security to foreigners of every nation, whatever their antecedent politics. 28 March: Abolition of the punishment of flogging in the army and navy. 24—25 March : Judicial and fiscal reforms. 29 March : Legal equality between citizens of all religions.

the enemy.   All the Venetian provinces were in
arms.   The movement reached the recesses of
Frioul on the 23rd: and the important fortress
of Palma-Nuova was abandoned without a
struggle during a panic of the garrison and
commander.

A serious check cast everywhere a shadow
over these happy beginnings.   During the night
of the 22nd and 23rd of March, the ephemeral
governmental commission established the previous evening, had a moment before dissolving,
committed a fault which Manin could not
repair.

Nothing could be of greater importance to
Venice than the securing of the Austrian fleet
moored in the port of Pola, in Istria.   Although
Austrian by name, it was strictly Venetian, and
manned by Venetians and Dalmatians.   This
little squadron would have unhesitatingly responded to any appeal from Venice.   The commission decided upon immediately sending to
Pola the only steam-boat at hand, which performed the service between Venice and Trieste
for the Austrian *Lloyd's* company.   The ex-
governor, Count Palffy, who had promised to

depart as quickly as possible from the city, asked
to be allowed to take his passage in this steamer.
This, at any cost, ought to have been refused :
but the extreme ease with which their deliverance had been effected, as Madam Manin wrote,
a few days afterwards, had turned the wisest
heads, and inspired a foolish confidence. Notwithstanding the representations of Mengaldo, the
commander of the civic guard, permission was
given to Count Palffy to embark, and the captain
of the steamer had orders to convey him to Trieste, after delivering his despatches at Pola. No
sooner were they at sea, than Palffy and his
followers intimidated the captain, and compelled
him to steer direct for Trieste. Instead of the
Venetian despatches reaching Pola, it was the
Austrian. The forts of Pola were turned upon
the squadron, and their batteries prevented the
ships from leaving the port. Thus, the opportunity was lost for ever. Out of eleven ships of
war, two only, which were at sea, ever reached
Venice. If this fleet had been taken, any
attempt on the part of Austria to blockade
Venice would have been impossible, whatever
had been the chances of war. Venice would

have blockaded Trieste, and perhaps have taken
Pola and Fiume, and roused Istria and Dalmatia to revolt, where the most ardent sympathy
prevailed.*

The glorious news from the mainland prevented the Venetian people from feeling the full
·loss they had sustained by this maritime failure.
On the 25th of March certain tidings arrived of
the triumph of the Milanese. A city of 160,000
souls, without organization, and almost without
arms, after five days of carnage, had driven from
its walls an army of upwards of 15,000 men,
commanded by the Austrian general-in-chief, Radetsky, in person.† The savage atrocities com-

---

* *Relation du Captain Maffei*, ap. *Gazetta di Venezia,*
of the 15th April. *Ricordi degli Antoni.*—Another
account, by Count Comello; MS.

† Radetsky had at first, in Milan, more than ten
thousand men, ten battalions, five squadrons, twenty-
four pieces of cannon (besides those in position in the
citadel), and he was reinforced by all the neighbouring
garrisons except two battalions which were made prisoners at Monza and Como by the insurgents of the
small villages and country. (See the official state of
the Austrian army in A. de La Forge, vol. i. p. 359.)
The political indifference of the Lombard rural districts

mitted by the Austrian soldiers served only to raise the ardour of the insurrection without inducing reprisals which would have sullied its triumphs.*

has been much exaggerated. In the first phase of the national struggle, the peasants rose in thousands around Milan, Como, Mantua, &c.   They went very resolutely to the assistance of Milan, and greatly contributed to compelling the Austrians to retreat, by cutting off the supplies of provisions.

According to the Italian accounts, a thousand citizens of both sexes and of all ages perished at Milan. The loss of the Austrians was four thousand men. The " days of Milan," it must be said to the honour of the Italians, formed a noble struggle, or rather the most splendid series of street-fights that had been seen since the commencement of the French Revolution. A population five times less than that of Paris in 1830, defied a *corps d'armée* superior to the troops that vanquished the Parisians in July.   Paris, in fact, had a serious encounter with only ten thousand guards—the few regiments of the line present in July sympathised very little with the Bourbons, and took only a slight part in the struggle.

* The notorious Count Bolza, chief of the police, a legitimate object of hatred, was not even ill-treated by those who took him. For the Austrian barbarities see a letter from M. Cæsar Cantu, in the *Raccolta di tutti gli atti*, etc., vol. i. p. 475, and the work of M. de la Varenne, *les Autrichiens et l' Italie*, p. 217-220, 8vo. 1858.

Radetsky retired in fearful disorder, and the
several Austrian corps seemed as if submerged
in the waves of a stormy sea.   All Lombardy
rallied round Milan : all Venetia round Venice.

On the 24th March, the Venetian government proclaimed equality of laws between the
city and its old provinces, and announced that
the constitution of the Venetian Republic must
be the united task of the deputies of the entire
state.*   All the provinces except Verona, which
was still occupied by the enemy, responded by
sending their adhesion to Venice.   On the 31st of
March a new decree invited the provincial committees to elect three councillors each, to form a
council near the Venetian government, pending
the meeting of the constituent assembly.   Tommaseo desired greater privileges for the provinces.
He asked that their delegates should form part of
the government.   In the ordinary state of things,
this would only have been just—but, during

---

* " The example we shall give is, before everything
that of moral and social reforms (more important even
than political forms), and that of an eqality, not sub-
versive, but just and religiously observed."—*Raccolta*,
etc. vol. i. p. 96.

a revolutionary crisis and war, to put the power into the hands of a committee of twenty-five persons would have been the ruin of everything—and therefore Manin would not consent to it.

A vigorous unity must not be allowed to become relaxed—nor must we sleep upon a first success. For a moment there was hope that Lombardo-Venetia would free herself by a single effort, unaided by the rest of Italy. In the impetuosity of the first days of success, it seemed as if the two great *places d'armes* of the ex-kingdom would be as fortunate as the other cities. There also the people had risen *en masse*, under the tricoloured standard; and, had the Veronese and the Mantuans evoked, if not such a statesman as Manin, at least men capable of directing and sustaining the movement, success would have been possible at Verona, in spite of the numerical strength of a garrison paralysed by the fears of the viceroy, and anarchy in the command. At Mantua success seemed certain. The garrison was nearly all Italian, and the forts and citadel might have been taken almost without a blow. Verona and Mantua lost, Radetsky could but flee into the Tyrol without his army. The loss of Mantua, even without Verona, had been sufficient to change the whole of the military operations.

Men, very disastrously for their country—at Verona it was the municipality, at Mantua the bishop—interfered, negociated, and deluded the people with idle words. Important time was lost: the threatened garrisons were reinforced by Croats and Germans, who abandoned the neighbouring cities; and Verona and Mantua again fell under a foreign yoke.

The war was now in Lombardo-Venetia: the enemy held places of refuge. In this war the whole of Italy, people and governments, appeared to concur together. The youth of Genoa and of Turin flew to arms, on hearing of the insurrection of Milan. Albert, after a few days' hesitation, comprehending that the honour of his house and the future of his crown would be lost, if he did not act, took the bold step of entering Lombardy at the head of his army. The Grand Duke of Tuscany, Austrian as he was, dared not refuse to authorise by his proclamations the march of the Tuscan volunteers

to the Po.   Other volunteers set out from Rome ;
and the Pope's regular troops proceeded from Bologna to Ferrara, under the command of General
Durando. Naples responded to the appeal. King
Ferdinand, or, rather, the liberal ministry to which
circumstances had compelled him to submit,
promised the support of all his land and naval
forces.   Finally, as if in response to the voice
which began to demand an Italian representative
assembly superior ' to all local governments,
the national party everywhere imposed on these
governments the unity of the flag, the tri-coloured
standard of the Italian revolution.

 Should Italy attempt to rely solely on her own
strength ?   The opinion of Manin, as we have
seen, upon this all-important point, was perfectly
settled.   Manin could not admit that a question
of life and death should be determined by sentiments of national pride, or by an exaggerated
point of honour.   It was impossible ,that Italy
in arms, and valiantly fighting her own battles,
could be, as in 1796, like a lifeless corpse, the
passive object of contention between France
and Austria.   He had no apprehension of interference on the part of France, except as their

auxiliary.   Manin knew well, that it was not on
the Italian side of the Alps that France had any
wish to urge territorial claims.   Therefore he
entertained no alarm of the consequences of the
interference of France.   He believed that the
interests of the French republic, and the Italian
revolution, were too closely identified for that
interference to be withheld.

From the 23d of March, the French Vice-Consul had assured the Venetian government that
he had no doubt of being immediately authorized by the provisional government of France to
acknowledge the new Republic.   On the 28th,
Manin, as President of the Venetian provisional
government and Minister of Foreign Affairs, noti-
fied the reconstruction of the Venetian Republic
to the Italian cabinets, and to those of Paris and
London.   In his letter to the French government, he thanked France by anticipation for a
support " which gave much cause for hope and
none for fear."   " The aid of a country of which
Lamartine is minister cannot be dangerous."*

* *Raccolta, &c.* vol. i. p. 354.   The letter to the
English minister (Lord Palmerston) was very skilfully
written.   No man knew better how to adapt his lan-

Two days afterwards (30th March), Manin
guage and style to the character of the men and people
he addressed.

"*The Provisional Government of Venice to Lord
Palmerston.*

"*Venice, 28th March.*

"*To the Secretary for Foreign Affairs of Great Britain.*

"The Provinces of the ancient Venetian State, in assuming the title of Republic, believe themselves faithful
to the past and obedient to the necessities of the present.   A nation like England, in which respect for tra-
dition is a kind of religion, will feel how sacred the past
must be to the Provinces.   A constitutional government
in this country, in the present state of its mind, would
have proved only an inconvenient and dangerous transition, and the revolutionary cause would have been followed by a despotism worse than that from which it has
escaped.   We believed that the only means of remaining
independent consisted in being free ; but the same feeling
that prompted this resolution imposed on us respect for
every established government.   We entertain no doubts as
to the sentiments of that great nation where the love of
liberty is an instinct, and which, by the grandeur of its
aims, and the perseverance with which it has maintained
them, reminds us more than any other of the success
and glory of ancient Rome.   The Venetian flag, when
it encounters the British on the sea, will always, we
hope, receive a friendly salute.

" For the Provisional Government of the Venetian
Republic,　　　　　　　　The President, MANIN."

wrote a second letter to M. Lamartine, Secretary for Foreign Affairs to France :—

" By a circular, addressed to your diplomatic agents (4th of March), you declared that the treaties of 1815 had legally ceased to exist, and that the territorial boundaries of these same treaties *can no longer be admitted except as matters of fact.* Now, with respect to the Venetian territory, *the fact no longer exists. In the decrees of Providence, the hour of re-construction for the oppressed nationality of Italy has sounded."* *

Tommaseo, a member of the Venetian government, and personal friend of M. de Lamartine, had added to Manin's dispatch a letter, in which he requested of the French minister an immediate supply of muskets and the purchase of a vessel of war.† Two Venetian agents immediately started for Paris to negociate this business.

Tommaseo received a private reply from M.

---

* Alluding to a phrase in M. de Lamartine's circular on the eventual intervention of France in favour of oppressed nationalities.

† *Documents inédits.*

de Lamartine, dated the 18th of April, full of expressions of sympathy for Venice and Italy; but the Venetian government received no official reply.* A new Consul-General for France, M. Limperani, arrived at Venice, but without special instructions. This consul could only express to the Venetian government his very warm personal sentiments for the Venetian cause, and the sympathy of public opinion in France. "It is well known," he said to Manin, "that the sympathy of France, when she possesses liberty of action, is never without results."

"I hope," replied Manin, "that the united efforts of the different Italian States, that the ardour which animates the people of the Peninsula, will suffice to expel the enemy, if not, we shall have recourse to the generosity of France. Meanwhile, we should be glad to see at once some French vessels in the Adriatic, and I beg,

* His agents at Paris wrote to say, that they had no hope of being able to buy a steamer of the government, and that the twenty thousand muskets could be had for ready money only, which would involve very vexatious delays. (Letters of Nani and Zanardini to Manin, from the 9th to the 11th of April. MS.)

Citizen Consul, that you will lose no time in communicating our wishes to the minister of foreign affairs."*

This request was very far from expressing all that Manin wished for; we shall soon discover what were the circumstances that compelled him thus to limit demand for support. This request, and that for the official recognition of the Venetian Republic, were reiterated several times, and strongly supported by the consul, in a series of despatches, in which M. Limperani showed to what extent Venice and the men who governed her were deserving of the sympathy of France, and presented a powerful point of support to French policy. It cannot be said that the French government was kept in the dark by its agents at Venice, as they were at some other points. France was very efficiently represented at Venice, during the whole of the war in Italy, and nothing more could have been wished for, than to see the advice of our consul attended to at Paris.

The interest and the duty of France seemed

* See the despatches of the 12th and 15th of April, in A. de la Forge, vol. i. 332, 358.

completely identical, as far as related to the recognition and protection of the Venetian republic. With the French republic.it was not a mere
matter of taste, it was one of strict obligation
to repair the wrong of Campo Formio—to lay
down on its inauguration a policy different from
that of the government it displaced. This was
but to assert its own title to exist. That policy
ought to have been an open and avowed opposition to the Austrian monarchy, the natural
enemy of the principle of nationality which the
French revolution represented. In order fully to
understand the results which falsified every appearance and every anticipation, and which led
to such fatal consequences to European liberty
and nationalities, we must take a survey, from
an international point of view, of the parties
and the leading influences which at this time
manifested themselves in France and in Italy.

Two systems of policy directly opposite were
then contending for mastery in France; the first
was that of an armed propagandism, the second
was that of peace, and the maintenance of
friendly relations with all the governments ex-
isting in Europe on the 24th of February. In our

humble opinion neither one nor the other was
right. The first, in attempting to impose democratic revolution on other countries, at the point
of the bayonet, would only have turned against
France the populations she desired to excite to
revolt. These populations were for the most part
disposed to rise of their own free will, and on their
own account, imitating the example but not compelled by the coercion of France. The second policy
was wrong in seeking to confine France to herself—in restricting her from influencing Europe
—except, as it was said, by the example of free
institutions and by negotiations—and by forbid-
ding her not only from exciting national revolutions against the dynasties of 1815, but even
from supporting those which arose spontaneously.
The second assumed to impose on France a part
which, perhaps, would have been very well
suited for England or the United States, but
which was directly opposed to the spirit of the
French nation, and which made the 24th of February a catastrophe without motive or object. It
must inevitably have destroyed at home the liberty it aimed at securing. On the one hand,
it would have handed over France to the rage of

its own passions, strongly inflamed by the revolution and driven back upon themselves in useless
fury, for want of any suitable or noble occupation
of their energy.* On the other hand, the result
must have been the suppression of all kindred
revolutions : France would have been crushed
by the double imputation of selfishness and weakness, each equally fatal, and been disarmed in the
face of that spirit of reaction, which, when victorious in other countries, would in turn have
invaded France, enfeebled and demoralized by
its own internal discord.

Public opinion did not sustain the propagandist
system in its imprudent and unfortunate attempts
on the French frontier : it equally declared itself against the pacific system, which, however,
would not have dared to make any open manifestation in the case of an appeal addressed to the
arms of France by the insurgent people of Italy.

The provisional government, persuaded as they
were that a vigorous demonstration abroad was

* If we had had *days* of May on the Adige, would
we have had the *days* of June on the Seine ? .... "The
French republican Government," wrote the English Ambassador, Lord Ponsonby, " must have war to sustain
itself." This was clearly seen abroad.

equally essential both for the Republic and for
France, would not have waited for any pressure
from Paris before it acted. On the 6th of March
the Minister of Foreign Affairs, Lamartine, had demanded the immediate formation of four armies,
one of them consisting of fifty thousand men,
to be ready to proceed to Italy. Garnier-Pages,
the Minister of Finance, had declared that the
supplies should be forthcoming. On several occasions, Arago, the Minister at War, held himself
in readiness to respond to an appeal he expected.*

* Our information is derived from an analysis of the
secret committees of the provisional Government, made
at the present time by one of its members, M. Garnier-
Pages, who desires it to be published. On the 12th of
March, the energetic minister of finance opened a first
war credit of 114 millions of francs. On the 27th, the
National Italian Association, formed at Paris and presided over by Mazzini, who prepared to set out for
Milan, presented itself to the provisional government.
M. de Lamartine *offered the sword of France to Italy.*
Mazzini replied that he hoped Italy would *suffice for
herself.* (Moniteur, 28th of March.) At the end of
March, M. de Lamartine said to General Pepe, on his
starting for Naples, that France was ready to send a hundred thousand men to Italy. Pepe did not refuse them,
but said thirty thousand would do.

Unfortunately for Italy, unfortunately for France, the appeal was not made!

An extensive and fierce agitation against having recourse to the aid of France spread throughout Italy. The radical difference which separates the culpable appeal to the stranger in civil struggles, from the very natural appeal to external friends against foreign tyranny, was not attended to. In the great awakening of the oppressed nationalities, which burst forth in 1848, from the strong sense of their individuality, they did not comprehend the necessity for union. They attacked separately their common enemy, the *régime* of 1815, or even inflicted injuries on each other, to its profit. This was the principal cause of their reverses. To speak only of Italy ; among a great number of those who opposed the acceptance of foreign assistance, there was in that opposition a mixture of generous and thoughtless feelings— among some a blending of a systematic hatred and a rancour which had some foundation in the former wrongs inflicted by France, with apprehensions not so well founded ; in fine, political passions and interests among those who dreaded the republican spirit and the French parties— while all were united in hating the Austrians.

This last was peculiarly the moral position of a man who was about to play the principal part in the war of Italy—a man who has been, and who must be variously judged—the unfortunate King of Sardinia. We shall not disturb his memory by bitter words ! He died for his country. The devotion of his last days nobly expiated the errors of his life ; and his last consolation was to foresee, with the prophetic glance of the dying, a better future, the germs of which, fertilized by his misfortunes, would grow upon his grave. As Manin, the great exile of Venice, has said to the writer, as we were looking on the portrait of Charles Albert—who in its presence could still harbour a resentment ? Who could fail to experience a painful emotion at the aspect of that face, furrowed with so many griefs, agitated by so many troubles and painful uncertainties, tormented and torn between so many contrary impulses ? Compromised, upon entering life, by a fault and a misfortune which brought upon him the hatred both of Austria and of the Revolution—domineered over by the Jesuits' party, who by imposing on his strong devotional feeling associated him with all reactionary move-

ments abroad, and drove him at home to treat
with cruel severity (mingled with secret remorse)
his early friends, the confidants of the generous
purposes of his youth—yet retaining through all
in the depths of his heart the courage and traditional ambition of his house, he united a sincere passion for Italy with a profound aversion for
its German oppressor. Suddenly he found himself, by the impetuous course of events, torn from
the arms of Jesuits and absolutists, and thrown
into those of patriots and liberals, and placed at
the head of a revolutionary war, with Austria in
front, and the French Republic with socialism in
the rear ! We may imagine the chaos of all the
elements of the past and the future, amid which
this undecided spirit struggled, which became resolute only in presence of the enemy's cannon !
In this lies the secret of so many contradictory
words and actions, which cast upon him the imputation of perfidy before the halo of his self-
sacrifice and death had covered all.

A mutual distrust, as unavoidable as it was la-
mentable, separated Charles Albert from the republicans of France and Italy. The French republicans were persuaded that he attacked Austria only

for the purpose of appropriating Milan to himself, when Milan had freed itself without him, then making terms at the cost of Venice, and finally turning against France. He, on his side, believed that, if the French made a descent, it would be, as far as he was concerned, to trample on him, and to overthrow his kingdom. Under the most favourable circumstances, he was convinced, not without reason, that France would never consent that he should become King of Upper Italy while he remained Duke of Savoy; and he had not sufficient political courage, nor was he so exclusively Italian, as to sacrifice his old heritage to a new destiny. He began by the most obstinate protests addressed to the French government, not only against the intervention of France, but even against the formation of a simple corps of observation on the French frontier—a corps which appeared to him as sure to become the Italian army of reserve; and in the proclamation in which he announced the entry of his army into Lombardy, he uttered those words, since become so famous—" God had placed Italy in a position to be sufficient to herself."*

So far from seeking the counsel, encourage-

* *Fara da sè* (23rd March).

ment, or even the eventual support of France, he did not even give notice of his enterprise to the provisional government which he had never officially recognised. The correspondence of the Marquis of Pareto, Minister of Foreign Affairs to Sardinia, with the Marquis of Brignola, Piedmontese Ambassador at Paris, and his conversations with the English Ambassador at Turin, Sir R. Abercromby, are filled with his fears and mistrust of France.   Even the friendly conduct of the French government, at the period of the disturbance in Savoy, in the beginning of April, in no respect changed these dispositions.

On the 11th of April, M. de Lamartine wrote as follows to M. Bixio, French Ambassador at Turin :—" The events that have occurred in Italy occasion us so much anxiety as to induce us to contemplate the possibility of the descent of a corps of observation upon Piedmont, with the previous consent of the Sardinian government, or even, if necessary, without waiting for this consent. Endeavour to ascertain, indirectly, if, in the event of a *corps d'armée* marching through Savoy, the forts on the road to Maurienne will fire upon them."

M. Bixio replied, on the 15th of April, that

the intervention of France, unless asked for,
would be regarded by all parties as an act of
bad faith.   The commanders of the forts would
energetically defend them.   Intervention at the
present time would have the same effect upon
Italy, as the surprise of 1808 had upon Spain.
On the 20th of April, he again urged:—" The
essential character of the movement that agitated
Italy, and which profoundly distinguishes it from
all previous movements, is—that it is pre-emi-
nently Italian."   And he summed up all his
dispatches with saying, " Do not anticipate the
appeal.   Wait, and it will be sure to come !"

Charles Albert was, therefore, quite opposed
to an appeal to the French, as Venice was entirely favourable to it.   This sensible people, the
only one in Italy which had a legitimate and
terrible grievance against the new France, was
just the only one superior to any anti-French
prejudice, as well as to any Italian presumption.
The question depended on Lombardy.   If it
called upon France and joined Venetia, the
French provisional government would have
responded to the appeal, and Charles Albert
been obliged to choose between an alliance with
France and one with Austria.

Milan was divided. The heads of the citizens with the artisans, the *Cattaneo*, and *Cernuschi*, &c., whose heroism had accomplished the revolution prepared by the legal struggles of the aristocracy—wished for the French alliance, and the Lombardo-Venetian Republic. The aristocracy wished for the union of Lombardy to the constitutional monarchy of Piedmont. They rejected the French because Charles Albert rejected them.* These were the two most

* His first idea was not to reject them. The 27th March, the Lombard Provisional Government wrote to the French Provisional Government in the following terms :—" We have thought that we could address to the Provisional Government of the French Republic the expression of our respect and our sympathy. . . . It is for this Government, which has so solemnly declared that it would come to the assistance of all oppressed nationalities, and hasten their deliverance—it is for the government of the bravest and most generous nation of the world to find the means of aiding us in our present difficult circumstances.

" *Vive la Republique Française! Vive l' Italie Independante!*

"(Signed) CASATI, BORROMEO, &c. &c."

Charles Albert lost no time in obliging the Lombard Government to disavow its letter, under the pretext of explaining it.

important parties—between which there was no
room for a third. A third nevertheless appeared. This was the republican party, which
wished neither for Charles Albert nor the
French! and this impossible party had the misfortune to shelter itself under a name then possessed of great authority—the name of a man
who had acquired great influence in all parts of
Italy by his eloquent writings, by his indefatigable
intrigues, and that spirit of absolute nationality,
which, by reacting with extreme energy against
the old habit of local egotism, of *separation*,
made of him, to all intents and purposes, the
representative of the whole Italy, and not of
this or of that province. Jealous of the French
Revolution, and dreaming, in his patriotic pride,
not only of deliverance, but also of the moral
and political supremacy of the Italy which twice
before had ruled the world, Mazzini repeated
the *Fara da sè* with more energy even than
Charles Albert himself. But among all his
great faculties, he seldom had that of distinguishing a dream from a reality.

Under these circumstances, what could France
do? She could not cross the Alps in spite of

Piedmont and Lombardy. She ought (such is our profound conviction) then immediately to have recognised the Venetian Republic, as a reparation for *Campo Formio*, and as a practical denial of the treaties of 1815, denied in argument in the manifesto of M. de Lamartine. But it was not done. The French Republic, which would have done anything required by Italy united, would not do the little asked of it by a portion of Italy. Must we then suppose that there was some design in the French Government unfavourable to Venice, some thought of negociating with Austria as the expense of Venetian independence? We can positively assert that such a thought was never—we will not say discussed—but never hinted at by any person in the consultations of the provisional government.* All its discussions relating to Italy breathed only of a *unanimous* desire to cross the Alps. But did they all wish them crossed for the same purpose, with the view of the complete emancipation of Italy?

The majority of the Provisional Government were of opinion that it was precisely because they wished to treat with Italy as a whole against

* See note at end of Volume.

Austria—because they wished to compel her in
some way to make a formal and general appeal
to the arms of France, that they should refuse
to listen to the partial appeal of Venice, and not
insist upon the Minister of Foreign Affairs re-
cognising the Venetian Republic.   If Venice had
demanded an immediate armed intervention, this
intervention would have been heartily granted
by the majority of the Provisional Government ;
but, in this case, we believe that the Minister of
Foreign Affairs would only have yielded against
his own convictions to the wish of the majority.

Venice asked but little, and that little she
could not obtain; but, amid her convulsions,
and dreams of a great future, she did not then
feel the consequences of the refusal.   This little
was, in fact, a great deal.   It would have been
a step towards engaging France in the Italian
cause.   The recognition of the Venetian Republic by the United States and by Switzerland
was only the recognition of a fact : by France it
would have been something more—a promise.
What was wanted was to engage France at any
price.

This was just what the Minister of Foreign
Affairs wished to avoid—not from timidity, (for

moral courage was no less strong in him than
courage by temperament)—but from system. He
wished to cross the Alps as much as anyone, but
only as a means of imposing peace, and dic-
tating its conditions.   To shelter Venice against
Austria, would have been war.   M. de Lamartine did not desire the true war—a war of Nationalities.*   He had not that absolute and un-
compromising faith in the principle of nationality,
which, in our eyes, is the soul of Revolution.
Splendidly representing the ideas of liberty, of
humanity, and moderation in internal government, he did not inflexibly represent, in foreign
politics, the new law—the law of *nations* against
states.   M. de Lamartine had not wholly dis-
engaged himself from that world of the past
which he had renounced, to bring to the Republic
his great genius and name.

* We quote the testimony of M. de Lamartine himself,
in the *Conseiller du Peuple*, in the *Histoire de la Revolution de* 1848; in the discussion in 1858, between M. de
Lamartine and M. Bastide, and Count Cavour and
General de la Marmora.   We should add, that M.
Garnier-Pages, in his unpublished work, does not admit
that M. de Lamartine followed this policy during the
first days of the Revolution of February.

It was a very great misfortune that the profound difference which existed on this point between his colleagues and himself was not sooner revealed, and that his colleagues had not been inspired to demand the immediate recognition of Venice. The consequences of such a recognition would have in part compensated for the baleful *Fara da sè* of Turin and Milan. It is a painful recollection, which ought to be less the reproach of the past than a lesson for the future. The foreign duties and interests of France do not change like its internal constitutions.

The armed intervention of France, which was refused by Piedmont and Lombardy, a refusal which compelled Venice to put off her demand for it, might have been postponed, perhaps, without imminent peril to the Italian cause, if Italy, which in its first days had soldiers, had also had generals. Lombardo-Venetia, as we have shown, could have freed itself (not to say defended itself) alone, if it had not been for the mistakes of Verona and Mantua. Charles Albert, in his turn, could have conquered alone, if he had pushed forward against the enemy, and thrown troops, regulars, and volunteers upon the Austrians, without giving Radetsky time to reconnoitre. From the letters of the Austrian officers, we may learn the situation of their army during the first days of April, that is from eight to fifteen days after the evacuation of Milan.

"You cannot imagine a more desolating spectacle! Carts full of wounded; here, a dragoon wearing the cap of a foot-soldier; there an artilleryman with the helmet of a dragoon, or the coat of a civilian: another without any coat at all: all these unfortunates under a pelting rain, which increased the disorder, passed the night in the open air, covered with blood and mud. It was impossible to recognise the colour of any uniform. For many days, our horses have not seen oats. Radetsky and all our veterans say that they never saw anything like it in any war."[*]

"Our frightful situation grows worse every day. Age and his reverses have turned Radetsky's head. Yesterday evening he again sum-

---

[*] Letter dated Castiglione, 1st April, to a German newspaper, quoted in *Archivie triennale della cose d' Italia*, vol. vi., p. 352, and Montanelli's *Memorie sull' Italie*, vol. 11, ch. xxxvii.

moned us to an extraordinary council, and for
the hundredth time repeated his proposal to fight
a great battle (with Charles Albert), or to cross
the Mincio and the Adige and join Nugent and
Giulay. Each of these propositions had very
warm advocates; but no one would give up his
opinion, and hence came reproaches, as usual.
Perceiving the great discord that prevailed, Radetsky grew furious, and cried out in French,
'You act like those fools of the Aulic council
who lost Italy by always wishing to wait. This
Italian rabble will end by massacreing us.'

"After which he went out, and rode on horse-
back for three hours, shouting to himself like a
maniac. And yet this man, who spoke to us
with so much passion, knows nothing of our
condition: he knows not what wounds gnaw us,
or that everything is in a state of destruction
among us. Fancy to yourself, my dear friend,
that there are not two officers here who agree
together; that the most foolish, hazardous, and
even the most disloyal projects are deliberated
upon. In certain cabals they speak of going over,
with a great many soldiers, to the Piedmontese;
in others, of arresting Radetsky, and sending him

to the advanced posts of the Italians.   These
propositions, at which every man of honour
should shudder, nevertheless find supporters.
All the ties of duty and discipline are relaxed or
broken.   The few men of integrity which still
remain have nothing left but to flee from this
sullied camp or die.

"I have taken my resolution.   Here nothing
can remain but dishonour : therefore I wish to
go, so that my honour may abide with me.   If
I remain, I must either participate in the infamous desertion of the army, or, perhaps, what is
still more infamous, in the arrest of our old
general.   It is my conviction that the Piedmontese will quickly attack us.   We shall not
defend ourselves.   The soldiers would throw
down their arms, and render themselves prisoners.   Rather than witness this, I would blow
my brains out.   We have attended the obse-
quies of the empire ! Who, two years ago, could
have said this to Metternich?" *

* Intercepted letter of the 1st of April, published in
the *Raccolta*, vol. i. p. 510. Admitting that there is
some exaggeration in it, the reality was certainly very
serious.

They used to boast of the firmness of the Austrian army after reverses. It had often been beaten, but never routed. The power of discipline like a chain of iron maintained the cohesion of its very heterogeneous elements; but as these elements, instead of being the parts of a machine, were clothed with living bodies, and as the various races in the machine of the empire were roused and struggled, it seemed on the point of learning what, under misfortune, would become of this army without nationality, and without any tie but a flag, which to the French, English, or Russian soldier is an inviolable personification of country, but a vain and abstract idol to the soldier of an empire which is not a nation.

The perusal of these documents makes the heart thrill, when we think how near the cause of justice was in obtaining a complete triumph. We are pained to consider by what series of strategetic and political errors a king, who had the heroism of a soldier but not the genius of a captain, lost an irreparable opportunity, and allowed himself to prolong a campaign which might have been ended at a single blow.

How, through fear of the republican spirit, this king discouraged the popular rising, repressed the vigorous element of the volunteers and free corps, and reduced to the proportions of an ordinary war the conflict which, to possess any chance of success, must remain a revolutionary war, as he well knew it could not be decided by strategy. How, finally, the Lombard aristocracy, which, by praiseworthy efforts, had prepared the way for the Revolution, knew not how to control it ; and, after having removed the energetic men of republican sentiments, drew so little advantage from the great opportunity it had under its hands, and seconded so feebly, not from ill will, but from inexperience, the king it had appealed to !

CHAPTER IV.

The affair of the Lloyd's steamer—The Venetian Cru-
saders—The Lombard-Venetian Campaign—General
Durando and the Pope—The encyclical of the 29th
April—Check at Corunda—The Austrians twice re-
pulsed before Vicenza—Defection of the King of
Naples—Curtaboni and Goito—Fall of Venice and
Venetian Provinces.

To return to Venice, upon whom, alas! fell the
faults of others.   Manin and his colleagues neglected nothing to organize and fortify the city
and country ; and, if there were also some slight
errors, they could not be imputed to the government.*   Its chief resources consisted of 7,000

---

* General Ulloa, in his important *Memoirs*, reproaches
the men to whom Manin had specially referred military

civic guards at Venice and a proportional number of other corps in the cities of *Terra Firma,* 6,000 sailors and marines, and 4,000 Italian soldiers, who had abandoned the foreign flag,[*] well-supplied forts and arsenal, a few little armed craft, and ten millions of *lire* (£382,500), found in the public treasury. This sum permitted the removal of unpopular and immoral taxes,[†] which were suppressed or reduced, as a boon to the people from the new Republic.

A committee of defence on military questions was established on the 29th of March; ten battalions of *gardes mobiles,* amounting to 6,000 men, were raised, besides an artillery legion and

questions of having given too much attention to a purely defensive organization of the lagoon, and not enough to the reconstruction of an efficient navy. However that may be, there were no means of repairing the loss of the squadron.

[*] They could not be maintained in a body; so, for the most part, they were authorized to return to their provinces, where they served as a nucleus for the militia. Those that remained formed a corps of gendarmes.

[†] The lottery, capitation tax, the newspaper stamp, the entry fees upon fishing-boats were suppressed. The tax on salt was reduced to a third.

a *corps de gendarmerie ;* the provinces were each
authorized to expend the disposable funds and
receipts for their defence, and they were sent a
supply of arms, ammunition, and money also ;
they armed small craft and boats to protect the
lagoons ; but the loss of the squadron did not
permit them to retain possession of the sea.

The maritime relations gave rise to a characteristic incident. Trieste, after a very vigorous
liberal movement, had returned to the Austrian
side, as soon as it saw its rival, Venice, break
from the bondage of the Austrian empire. The
Lloyd's company of Trieste, however, in the
interests of commerce, had obtained from the
Venetian government permission to resume the
steam-boat service, which had been interrupted
for a few days. During the interval, the bad
treatment of the citizens of Venice and Chioggia
at Trieste, and also of the Venetian crews of the
two ships detained at Pola, then taken to Trieste,
had violently excited the people. When the
Lloyd's steamer entered the port of Venice (30th
of March), the crowd assembled tumultuously
beneath the windows of the government palace,

loudly demanding reprisals and the seizure of the steamer, and called for the government.

The President and his colleagues did not appear in a body at the windows, and the government made no response; but Manin, he responded to the appeal. He came out alone, and, putting himself at the head of a detachment of the civic guard, proceeded towards the *Piazetta*, the little square which communicates from the square of St. Mark to the grand canal, where the *Lloyd's* steamer was lying. The crowd followed him, and hushed itself to listen.

Manin began :—

"I speak to you now, perhaps for the last time; for no government is possible, if it must come to the public square every moment to justify itself. I will never submit to that. The steamer has come to Venice under the guarantee of the government: nothing will induce us to abandon it. I am quite ready to resign the power the people has confided to me; but so long as I retain it, I shall be as resolute in maintaining public peace and order as I was in overthrowing a powerful enemy..... Our enemies have shown themselves mean and cruel; but meanness or cruelty never made any one happy. The Republic has guaranteed private property, and the *Lloyd's* steam-boat is such. To seize it, therefore, would be an act of piracy. Do not diminish the well-merited renown of Venetian faith and hospitality. On the contrary, oppose yourselves vigorously to every act which attacks commerce, the soul and life of Venice. Any other conduct would be worthy of Austria. Leave that to Metternich! As for me, Manin, I shall never consent to it, even if it costs me my life!"

The people retired, crying, *Viva Manin! Viva la Republica!* and on the morrow a proclamation, signed by Manin and Tommaseo, reminded the Venetians, in the simplest and noblest language, that the citizens had other means of communicating their wishes and opinions to the government than by clamours in the public square :—

"We have not assumed the cares, labours, and fearful responsibility of government to sacrifice the dignity we maintained in our private life and in difficult times. Citizens, take your confidence, or, rather, that in those who govern you, from us at once, but respect yourselves!"

Such were the means by which this man directed the people, whom he never flattered or deceived. And this people, to the last, showed itself worthy and capable of being thus directed.*

The war, however, absorbed every other thought. Venice and the *terra firma* exhibited equal ardour. At the end of March, bands of volunteers had quitted the city for Verona, the decisive point in the struggle, where they reckoned upon finding the Piedmontese. A second departure took place on the 7th of April, with solemn forms and ceremonies, in which the traditions of the middle ages were mingled with the new spirit. The patriarch blessed the *crusaders* of St. Mark and liberty, who marched with priests in their ranks, and a banner bearing the image of the cross at the head of their columns. Manin accepted and favoured these reminiscences of the remote past with the feelings, not of a leader of a crusade, but of a Greek or Roman

* Manuscript account, written the same day by Gerlin, Manin's Secretary; Dispatch of Mr. Clinton Dawkins, the British Consul, of the 31st March; and the *Augsburg Gazette* of the 8th of April, 1848.—*Raccolta,* vol. i. p. 264.

politician in presence of the local traditions of his country; and to him St. Mark was the popular symbol of his Venice.

The people were intoxicated with this enthusiasm and excitement; but Manin never exaggerated its consequences. Powerful for resistance in its lagoons, he knew that the republic was feeble for a campaign in the field,—if, before being able to organize everything on a large scale, he should be obliged at once, with a few free corps, to defend the provinces against a fresh Austrian army. The fate, therefore, not of Venice merely, but of Venetia, depended on the aid supplied by the regular forces of the other Italian states, but especially on the first operations of Charles Albert. When Manin learned that Radetsky, after having retreated step by step, had vainly attempted with his demoralized army to dispute the passage of the Mincio—that the King of Sardinia, from the 8th to the 10th of April,* had repulsed him on the Adige —the heart of the Dictator bounded with de-

* From two to four days after the date of the intercepted letter, which showed the situation of the Austrian army to be desperate.

light. He had every reason to believe that the next courier would bring news of the utter defeat of the Austrians, and of the entry of the Piedmontese into Verona. In that event the Piedmontese would only need to march to the frontiers of Trento and Friuli, to close Italy against the corps of the enemy, which were forming in Carniola, Carinthia, and the Tyrol. These troops would arrive too late to succour Radetsky, and were too feeble to act without him. Then Venetia would have time to become disciplined and organized, under the protection of a victorious army.

But, instead of the hoped-for triumph, Venice learned that a few Austrian regiments had been allowed to quench the insurrection in the Italian Tyrol ;* and that Charles Albert, instead of pushing vigorously against Radetsky, and scat-

* Charles Albert dared not allow his troops to enter Trento, for fear of offending the Germanic Confederation, which had the presumption to treat Trento, an Italian province, as an annex of the Tyrol, a German province. —(See the *Memoirs* of Montanelli for a narrative of the movement at Trento, whither he himself hastened *incognito* from Tuscany, to excite the mountaineers of the Alps, heroically braving worse perils than those of the field of battle.)

tering his already beaten army, was wasting his
time in idle attempts upon Peschiera and Mantua.   When every day was worth a year, he
allowed the enemy three weeks to recruit on
the Adige.   When Radetsky found himself in
a condition to disturb Charles Albert in his
position before Peschiera, which the King was
making preparations to besiege, Charles Albert
attacked and carried the post of Pastrengo, on the
Adige (30th April), but neglected to drive the
enemy at once across the river.   It was only a
few days subsequently that he made an ill-pre-
pared *coup de main* upon Verona, which failed
(6th May).   Charles Albert continued to besiege
Peschiera.

The conditions of the campaign were wholly
changed.   Radetsky maintained his position before Verona.   General Nugent was advancing to
his aid by Friuli, the frontier of which he had
already crossed ; General Welden was on the
point of issuing from the Tyrol.   The only hope
for Venetia was now in the promised Roman
and Neapolitan contingents; for the aid promised by the Piedmontese government did not
arrive.   Charles Albert sent but one general to
Venice, one of the brothers Marmora, but no

troops (14th April). A first corps of regular pontifical troops and volunteers from Rome was at Ferrara, under the orders of General Durando.

The Venetian government had assured this corps all necessary supplies in material of war, money, provisions, and transports, to cross the Po, and operate upon Venetian territory. The general, however, did not advance; and his inaction astonished and irritated both the Venetians and his own soldiers. They did not know that the responsibility of this inaction was due to a higher authority than Durando. The Pope had forbidden his general from taking the offensive. And when Durando protested against the anomalous position in which he was placed, the Pope sent him an equivocal reply, which the general, who had an undecided character, hesitated to interpret as he might have done. The Roman ministry (for since the complex and illusory *Statuto* of the 14th of March there had been two governments at Rome) commanded Durando to place himself at the disposal of Charles Albert, the leader of the war. Charles Albert instructed Durando to come and support his operations on the Adige.

This was to abandon Venice. Manin, in a
very remarkable letter to Durando (18th April),
after energetically setting forth the moral reasons which protested against this desertion,
sagaciously predicted its military consequences.
These were, that the line of the Isonzo not being
defended, General Nugent would pass by, without besieging the fortifications of Palma Nuova,
" and proceed to concentrate his movements with
what remained of the Austrian forces in Mantua,
Peschiera, and Verona. This evidently is the
plan of the Austrians; and, as it is the only one
they can make in the present state of affairs,
they will overcome their habitual slowness to
put it into execution as quickly as possible." *

To prevent the success of this plan, to prevent
the junction of Nugent with Radetsky, was, in
fact, " the great question of the campaign," as
the Piedmontese general, La Marmora, well
understood. This is shown in his letter from
Venice to the Roman general, Ferrari, to press
him to march straight upon Friuli, with a
second Roman corps formed at Bologna (21st
April). Ferrari alone could not defend Venetia;

* Manuscript documents.

and the Venetian government decided upon
sending one of its members, the Minister Paleocapa, to the head-quarters of Charles Albert
in order to persuade him to aid vigorously
in intercepting the progress of Nugent (21st
April).

The nature of the instructions given to Paleocapa show that the military question was com-
plicated with a political one, and that the Venetian government suspected some mental reservation in the abandonment of Venetia, which, they
believed, would compel it to give itself up to
Charles Albert before he would assist it.

" If the King or his ministers inquire if we
are disposed to renounce the republican form,
what reply shall I give ?"

" That we shall accept such form of government as the nation shall decide upon."

" If the King inquires if we are decided upon
forming a single state with Lombardy, what
shall I say ?"

" Say, that if the Constituent Assembly de-
cides that this union must take place, we shall
accept it."

" If the King expresses any intention of form-

ing a single state of Northern Italy, with Milan
for its capital?"

"We are at the orders of the Constituent
Assembly."

"In case the King urges his already expressed
desire for the Venetian and Lombard provinces
to be represented by a single Assembly?"

"The first proposition of the Government
to the Venetian Assembly will be to ask if it
intends to unite itself with the Lombard Assembly." *

We see by this what position the Venetian
government assumed upon a question that occupied every mind. It held a legitimate reserve,
but rejected no solution the national wishes imposed on it. We shall again refer to the important question of fusion with Piedmont, and
to Manin's sentiments with regard to it. It
resulted from the mission of Paleocapa that
Charles Albert finally consented for Durando to
proceed to the Venetian provinces with all the
Roman auxiliaries (24th April). The marches
and countermarches of Durando caused a great
loss of valuable time. The Austrian general,

* A de La Forge, vol. ii. p. 71.

Nugent, following exactly the plan surmised by
Manin, had passed the Isonzo, masked Palma
Nuova, and on the 22d of April took Udine,
the capital of Friuli.   Passing the Tagliamento,
he reached Piave on the 30th.   It was only
upon this river, that is, in the very heart of
Venetia, that Durando with the Romans, and
Marmora with the Venetian *crusaders*, began to
dispute ground with the enemy. •

Meanwhile an event of immense importance
occurred at Rome.   The Pope, who at first
appeared to lend himself to the national movement, and from the Quirinal blessed the banners
of the pontifical troops and free corps about
setting out for the war of independence (23d
March), had ever since abstained from every act
which could further compromise him in this
direction, and was unwilling to give any instructions, or sign any order, relating to the war.
The Roman troops, at the moment they entered
the lists against the enemy, actually found themselves deprived of the rights of men, as no official act had declared a rupture between their
government and Austria.   It was already known
that the Austrians had hanged a Roman pri-

soner.   The ministers of the Pope energetically
demanded a declaration of war from Pius IX.
The German cardinals, on their part, intimated
to the Pope that this declaration would entail
their immediate separation from the Holy Chair ;
while a contrary declaration would effect the
restitution to the Roman church of all the privileges of which Joseph II. had deprived it
(25th April).[*]

Pius IX. made his decision, and, without
consulting with any one, pronounced, in the con-
sistory of the 29th of April, the famous allocution, in which he invited the Germans not to
require of him the impossible task of arresting
the ardour of those of his temporal subjects
who, sharing the hatred of all other Italians for
the German nation, wished to co-operate in
the common cause. . . . "As many are now
demanding that we should unite with the other
princes and peoples of Italy, to declare war
against Austria, we believe that it is our duty
to formally and strongly protest against such
a resolution, which is quite contrary to our
thoughts, seeing that, notwithstanding our un-

* *Venice*, by Edmund Flagg (1853).

worthiness, we occupy on the earth the place of
Him who is the author of peace—and that we
embrace every country, every people, in a general
feeling of paternal love."

So vanished, never to return, the dream that
had excited the passionate ardour of Italy and
the astonishment of Catholicity—the dream of
a pontiff-king personifying Italian nationality.
Thus was shown the absolute incompatibility between the duties of the chief of a religion which
embraces the world, and those of the political
head of a nation, or fragment of a nation.   At
the first step that Italy took to emancipate itself
by the force of arms, its guide abandoned it, and
declared that he embraced the country and its
enemy in one impartial love.

We may judge from this the true value of
those reproaches of ingratitude which have been
lavished on the Italians.   The union had existed
only in the false and the impossible; the first
shock of the reality dissolved it.

On the same evening the ministry tendered
their resignation.   Next day the people rose in
tumult; the civic guard fraternized with them,
the reactionary cardinals were besieged in their

palaces—the castle of St. Angelo was attacked.
The delegates of Lombardy, Venetia, and Sicily
addressed to the Holy Father a truly respectful
statement, an eloquent and pathetic remonstrance,
in the name of right and the principle of nationality, "The work not of men, but of God."
The Pope retracted, the ministry was recalled,
and strengthened by the addition of Count Ma-
miani, the old leader of the Romagnese and
Bolognese movement of 1831. An absurd
arrangement was concluded, according to which
the Pope was not to declare war against Austria,
but to write to the Emperor Ferdinand and invite him to evacuate Italy quietly, and he was
formally to authorize Durando to place himself
under the orders of Charles Albert, which that
general had, in fact, done several days previously.

A veil was thrown over the disastrous dis-
closure that had been made. The allocution
was attributed to a moment of aberration, to
perverse counsel. At Venice they continued
to invoke the name of Pius IX., but confidence once lost could never be restored,
and reflective minds clearly understood that
from that hour the radical rupture between the

pontiff-king and Italian nationality was only postponed, the catastrophe that followed six months afterwards was inevitable. This, unhappily, was not understood by France, absorbed in its intestine quarrels, for public opinion did not keep pace with the rapid progress of Italian affairs, hence the misunderstanding which prepared and rendered possible the deplorable war of the following year.

The Austrians grew bolder. On the 4th of May they proclaimed at Trieste the Maritime blockade of Venice. Through the unfortunate affair of Pola it was with Venetian ships that they presumed to blockade Venice! The menaced city expected the maritime succour of Naples and Sardinia. The Italian marine was anticipated by the French. The first friendly vessel of war which appeared before Venice was the steam frigate *Asmodée*, detached from Admiral Baudin's squadron, which had arrived in the harbour of Leghorn at the end of April.*

---

* It was at the request of M. Bixio, French Ambassador at Turin, that the admiral had despatched this frigate to Venice. M. Bixio desired to do more. "I do not know, *Monsieur l'Amiral*," he wrote on the 27th

The Austrians, desirous, above all things, of avoiding a collision with the French, did not venture to interdict the *Asmodée* access to the lagoon (10th May).

This was the response to one of Manin's requests, and it seemed a good omen for the rest. The people welcomed the French officers, who landed at the Piazzetta, with shouts of *Viva l'Italia! Viva la Francia!* * The frigate came, it is true, only as a friend, not as an avowed auxiliary, but Manin had not asked more, and he was the better satisfied, because his agent at Paris had begun to make him uneasy as to the disposition of the French government toward him.

Six days after the arrival of the French frigate, the Neapolitan squadron appeared in sight

of April, " what your instructions are, nor within what limits it is possible for you to *interfere forcibly;* but whatever they may be, I beg of you most earnestly to send immediately to the Adriatic as many vessels as you judge convenient to display the French flag." The admiral replied that he would send only one vessel.

* The Romans never reckoned more than fifteen thousand men, and this number was reduced by various detachments.

of Lido (16th May). The Sardinian squadron could not be long. The coming arrival was announced, of fourteen thousand men of the Neapolitan army, which, already preceded by the volunteers, advanced by the Romagna, and would be followed by a second corps of twenty-four thousand men. This good news balanced the effect of the untoward events of the Terra Firma. The two corps of troops, and the Roman volunteers, formed in all, with the Venetian *crusaders*, an army of operation of twenty thousand men, commanded by two unskilful leaders, the circumspect * Durando and the ardent Ferrari, who retarded, but did not delay effectually, the progress of General Nugent, who met them with forces somewhat less in number, but very superior in organization. On the 8th and 9th of May, Ferrari, with a fraction of volunteers and Roman troops, fought vigorously at Cornuda, against a part of Nugent's army. The enemy was reinforced ; Ferrari did not concentrate his too widely scattered forces, and was not aided by Durando, who, on his side,

* At least three-fourths of the Romano Venetian army were wholly inexperienced in the use of arms.

had various points to protect, he therefore had
to give way; during the retreat his troops became disordered; the remarks upon the too
famous encyclical of the 29th April demoralized
his Roman troops; he was obliged to retire
upon Trevisa, then upon Mestra, leaving Trevisa
guarded.

Durando, with his corps and the Venetian
crusaders, had retired upon the Brenta, with
the view of closing the road from Vicenza and
Verona against the enemy. Nugent made a
false attack upon Trevisa. Upon the entreaties
of the people, Durando abandoned his position
to return to the assistance of Trevisa, which
defended itself gallantly. Nugent left Trevisa,
passed the Brenta, and marched straight to
Vicenza. Durando followed the enemy. On
the night of the 20th and 21st of May, the
Venetian government was informed that Vicenza had been attacked by Nugent's advanced
guard. A battalion of the Roman national
guard, the civic guard of Vicenza, and some
Venetian and Lombard volunteers had defended
this open place valiantly against five or six
thousand of the enemy, but they fully expected

that the attack would be renewed by a much greater force. At six in the morning, on the 21st of May, Manin and Tommaseo, accompanied by General Antonini, Commander of Venice,* set out by railway with a reinforcement of a thousand men. The fight was resumed in the afternoon. The advocate and literary man who governed Venice showed that he cared little for the Austrian bullets. The courage of Manin, which on many occasions astonished the boldest, was of a peculiar nature—it was an absolute indifference to danger and death. It would have required a great effort of the imagination for him to comprehend the natural instinct of fear.

The fusillade and cannonade continued till nightfall ; the reinforcements brought from Venice had the honours of the day ; the brave General Antonini had his right arm carried away by a ball ; but Durando, by forced marches, had also arrived with four thousand regulars.† The

---

* Recently arrived from Paris with a troop of refugees, organized into a legion.

† The greater part were Swiss, in the pope's service.

Austrians beat a retreat, and Manin and Tommaseo returned to Venice next day at dawn.

Vicenza, Trevisa, and the neighbouring provinces of Venice appeared saved for the moment, but the enemy had none the less attained his principal object, the junction of Nugent with Radetsky. Durando did not consider himself strong enough to give battle to Nugent in the open country, to prevent his turning Vicenza and gaining Verona. Vicenza was not yet out of peril. Radetsky, furious at his lieutenant's having allowed himself to be repulsed at that place, made Nugent's corps immediately retrace its steps with reinforcements, and another general, La Tour et Taxis, with orders to take Vicenza at any price; for its importance to him was very great, on account of its position between the roads from Friuli and the Tyrol. On the night of the 23rd and 24th of May, Vicenza was assailed for the third time; but the besieged, animated by their previous successes, and well directed by Durando, displayed so much energy in the defence, as to break the violence of the attack. Forty-two pieces vainly cannonaded and bombarded the town from midnight until three in the afternoon of the next day; the sixteen thousand soldiers of La Tour et Taxis could not force the feeble barricades of Vicenza. Nugent's corps again retired in the evening of the 24th to Radetsky's camp.

The hearts of the Venetians swelled with hope and legitimate pride. The government increased its armaments, and decreed an impost of ten millions of lire (nearly four hundred thousand pounds), to be divided among the provinces unoccupied by the foreigner, under the form of a forced loan, guaranteed by railway shares in the railway from Venice to Milan, which had become national property (15th May).

The people anticipated the sacrifices demanded by the government. While the pope contended with his people to abandon the road upon which he had himself led Italy, the poor monks, his subjects, continued preaching the national crusade with fiery eloquence, and the Barnabites Ugo Bassi and Gavazzi, almoners of the Roman volunteers, were the most devoted and useful among Manin's auxiliaries at Venice. At one of their preachings the military

M 2

chest was enriched with a thousand pounds in
money, and an amount much greater in value
in plate, jewels, provisions, arms, and clothing.
The women gave their ear-rings, neck-chains,—
even the large silver bodkins with which they
adorn their long raven hair.   The poor brought
their beds for the use of the soldiers; condemned prisoners, even, sent their mite for the
service of the country; every one contributed
according to his resources.   Manin gave his
silver snuff-box, the only article of value he possessed; the brothers Bevilacqua gave their
house; Giacomo Treves gave a hundred thousand lire; Messieurs Giovanelli gave seventy
thousand; a young girl, whose betrothed had
been killed by the Austrians, brought her wed-
ding-ring as a gift.*

On the 22nd of May the Sardinian squadron
anchored before Venice; on the 23rd it united
with the Venetian and Neapolitan squadron,
and the combined Italian fleet compelled the
Austrian squadron to take refuge in the port of
Trieste, then summoned the Austrians to restore the vessels of war belonging to the repub-

* Flagg's *Venice*, vol. i. p. 426.

lic of Venice, vessels which constituted the bulk of the enemy's squadron.

A day of happy presage, but which had a gloomy morrow! Alarming news from Naples had begun to circulate on the 24th, the whole truth had become known. The 15th of May, an ominous day for European liberty, after a quarrel between Ferdinand and the Chamber, which seemed appeased by an arrangement, a partial and ill-timed insurrection had broken out. Stifled in blood and pillage, it restored to Ferdinand the power he had lost at the rising in January, and the first use he made of it was to abandon the Italian cause and despatch an order recalling his fleet and army. His previous instructions to the commanders of his land and sea forces were very similar to those given by Pope Pius IX. to Durando, interdicting the general from crossing the Po, and the admiral from attacking the Austrians without fresh orders.

Charles Albert, it must be admitted, had given the King of Naples a pretext by eluding the overtures made at the beginning of April by the Neapolitan minister, relative to a league

between the Italian states; the King of Sardinia did not wish to limit his ambition, and
accepted only a military co-operation, without
political conventions.

But for the catastrophe of the 15th of May,
General Pepe, the worthy veteran of Italian
liberty, and Admiral de Cosa, had certainly
guided the hand of the King of Naples; but
every thing was now changed. Little known as
a soldier (he had recently returned from an exile
of twenty-seven years), and not possessing those
brilliant qualities which suddenly attract and
carry away the masses, General Pepe did not
succeed in drawing his army into his generous
disobedience. The greater part of the Neapolitan troops obeyed the King's orders (27th
May).* Only two thousand men out of fourteen thousand obeyed their country's call, and
followed their old leader in Venetia.† Ad-

* Most tragical scenes occurred. One colonel, deserted by his regiment, blew out his brains; another
was struck by a fit of apoplexy.

† Among his two thousand men he had only one
battalion of regular infantry, a battery of artillery, and
a company of sappers. The remainder consisted of
volunteers.

miral Cosa soon afterwards sorrowfully set sail for Naples.

The defection of the Neapolitans more than compensated the Austrians for their check before Vicenza. Radetsky concluded that the time was come when he might resume the offensive against Charles Albert. He did not even await the arrival of a considerable reinforcement from the Tyrol. On the evening of the 27th, he set out from Verona with the bulk of his army. His plan was to send a detachment to throw provisions into Peschiera—to debouch upon Mantua with the main division of his army—defeat the Tuscan contingent, which watched rather than invested that place—attack the Piedmontese, whose lines were far too extensive, in the rear— seize upon their stores, and cut them off from Lombardy. On the morning of the 29th, the Austrians issued from Mantua in great force. The success of the plan seemed infallible.

But Radetsky had not foreseen that a handful of men, belonging to the free corps,* troops so

* According to Montanelli, there were scarcely five thousand Tuscans, three thousand of whom were volunteers, besides five hundred Neapolitan soldiers.—*Memoirs, &c.* vol. ii. c. xi.

scorned by military pride, would stop for a whole
day the progress of an entire army with its mass
of artillery.   The flower of the Tuscan youth
was cut down on that sad but glorious day.*
Montanelli, their eloquent professor and apostle,
who had become their leader in the fight, was
picked up for dead on the battle-field of Curta-
tone.   The Tuscans were crushed, but they had
saved the Piedmontese army.   The Austrians
were unable to advance until the following day,
and encountered the Piedmontese only on the
afternoon of the 30th.   They must have had
about thirty thousand men when they found
themselves face to face with the twenty thousand
Piedmontese, now drawn up between Goïto and
Ceresara.   But one of their divisions ordered to
turn the enemy's position arrived too late.   The
superior strategy of Radetsky failed against the
moral superiority of the Piedmontese soldiers.

* We cannot look without emotion, in the famous
Campo Santo of Pisa, on the monumental tablet which
consecrates the memory of these young heroes, who
died for Italy, most of them students of the university
of Pisa. This city of grand remembrances showed herself
worthy of her past, in raising this noble monument, in
troublous times, as a protest against Austrian reaction.

The Austrians were driven back with great loss upon Mantua. During the battle Charles Albert received news of the capitulation of Peschiera. The attempt of the Austrian right to throw supplies into this place had failed the day before; and Peschiera surrendered to the left wing of the Piedmontese.

Charles Albert, as well as his eldest son, the Duke of Savoy,* had displayed the greatest bravery in this action; but, as before, he neglected to improve his victory. The enemy retreated from the Mincio to the Adige, but he did not pursue him. He opposed no obstacle to Radetsky's receiving a reinforcement of sixteen thousand men, brought by General Welden from the Tyrol. And the 10th of June, eleven days after his defeat at Goïto, Radetsky was able to fall not only upon the Piedmontese, but also upon Vicenza, with forty thousand men and one hundred and eighteen pieces of artillery. He staked everything on this movement, for he ran the risk of being enclosed between the victorious army of Charles Albert and the ten or twelve thousand men who under Durando occupied Vicenza, or of losing Verona in taking Vi-

* Now Victor Emmanuel, King of Italy!

cenza, if Charles Albert should throw himself upon Verona, left without protection, and ready to rise upon the first signal from the Piedmontese.*

But Charles Albert, notwithstanding the intreaties of his Minister of War, Franzini, marched neither upon Verona nor upon Vicenza. He took Rivoli, to cut off communication with the Tyrol, after the Austrians had received every thing they had expected from the Tyrol; and when he at length set himself in motion to succour Vicenza, it was too late. After a heroic struggle of eighteen hours, the Austrians, at the price of fearful slaughter, took the heights that commanded the city on the south. Durando,, who had but one man against four, had to capitulate, in order to save the city from utter destruction. He undertook for his Roman and Swiss troops to evacuate the Venetian territory, and not bear arms against Austria for three months.

In the fall of Vicenza was included that of all the Venetian Terra Firma. The Venetian govern-

* The Veronese only awaited the signal, a large fire, which was to be lighted in the vicinity, and then they would have revolted.

ment was not in a position to defend Padua.
Trevisa and even the fortress of Palma Nuova,
blockaded for two months past, must soon capitulate; and, while Radetsky held Charles Albert
again in check between the Adige and the Mincio, the Austrians re-appeared in sight of the
lagoons!

Venetia had fallen, but all was not lost; for
Venice remained firm, resolved to fight against
arms and diplomacy to the last; for another evil,
more perilous than the first, now presented itself. This great peril was not an open attack
by force, which it would have been sure to repulse, but an European compromise, negociated
abroad, which sought to find a pretext for a new
Campo Formio in the fall of its provinces.*

A mitigated Campo Formio was, in fact, discussed in the diplomatic world even before the
fall of Venetia.

* The capitulation, promised to treat the inhabitants
mercifully. Radetsky kept his word in true Austrian
fashion, by exercising the most savage cruelty upon the
brave and unfortunate people of Vicenza. The Roman
government felt itself authorized to notice this conduct
in the enemy, by making its troops of the line occupy
the place. *The Pope refused!*

CHAPTER V.

Policy of the French and English Cabinets—Views of
M. de Lamartine—Lord Palmerston's Correspondence
—Mission of M. de Hummelaür to London—Nego-
ciations at Venice and Milan—Resolutions of the
French government—The 23d of June at Paris.

WE must now go back a few weeks, and trans-
port ourselves from Italy to England and France.

Manin had from the first believed he could
see the 'worst disposition on the part of the
English government. A secret struggle existed
at Venice between the French and English consuls; the one faithfully expressing the policy of
England in 1815, the other the policy of France
in 1848.* The English consul, Mr. Clinton

* This opposition did not change with the person of
the French consul, Limperani. M. Vasseur, who suc-

G. Dawkins, expressed himself very freely to Manin, when the latter spoke one day on the rights of nationalities.

" You ought to very well understand," replied Mr. Dawkins, " that my government cannot admit this right either for you or for Lombardy ; because, if it admits it, it would justify the rebellion of its subjects in India, the Ionian Islands, all the colonies, and Ireland even." *

This same consul, who kept a profound silence upon the barbarities committed on every occasion by the Austrian troops, wrote a declamatory letter to Manin, on the occasion of one of those rare acts of reprisal on the part of the Italian people, the murder at Trevisa, by the people and the Roman volunteers, in a day of suffering and wrath, of three prisoners, two of whom were Italians, accused of acting as spies for the enemy,

ceeded M. Limperani on the 10th of June, displayed the same feelings as his predecessor, and sustained them to the last with as much energy as political intelligence.

* See A. de La Forge, vol. ii. p. 37. The English consul had, with a jealous uneasiness, informed his government of the friendly advances addressed by the Venetian government to the Greek Ionians and to the Dalmatians and other Sclavonians.

and the third one of the directors of the sanguinary police of Modena.

Lord Palmerston, however, when the agents sent by Manin to France paid him a visit at London, showed quite a different attitude to that of his representative at Venice. He received the Venetians very graciously, and gave them to understand that the British government, although allied to that of Austria, would lend it no assistance, but would remain spectator.

The conduct and correspondence of Mr. Clinton Dawkins, ex-secretary to Lord Aberdeen, the friend of Radetsky, and an inveterate Tory, whom Lord Palmerston was wrong in allowing to remain in his place, has greatly contributed to the errors which prevail as to the principles and acts of the British Government with regard to Italy in 1848. An examination of the correspondence of Lord Palmerston will remove the prejudices that may exist on this subject. Lord Palmerston had no malevolent feelings either against Italy or France, and did not consider himself bound by the Tory logic of Mr. Dawkins on the score of nationalities. He had sincerely encouraged, through Lord Minto, the

liberal agitation of Italy in 1847. When the
Revolution of February broke out, he had doubtless some moments of anxiety and uncertainty
—he was afraid that the French Republic would
assume a character of universal propagandism,
that it would encourage the Chartist movement
in England, and yield to the solicitations of the
Irish repealers who came to Paris to invoke
the aid of France in exciting Ireland to
revolt. The policy of Lord Palmerston may at
first have been influenced by these apprehensions.
Before the insurrections of Milan and Venice,
he deterred Charles Albert from assuming the
offensive against Austria—but once the War of
Independence commenced, he was not hostile to
the national movement. He desired, at least at
first, that the French should not enter Italy—
but he did not at all desire that the Austrians
should remain there—and he wished, at heart,
that the military successes of the Italians, joined
to the fear of French invasion, and to the internal troubles of Austria, would oblige the
Austrians to evacuate the peninsula, for a pecuniary indemnity. Nothing can be more absurd
than to suppose that the British Cabinet was

ready at this period to make war upon France to
maintain in Italy the treaties of 1815. Lord
Palmerston did not even reply to Austria when
it appealed to him to support that iniquitous
compact. And it must be added, that public
opinion in England went beyond that of the
ministry, and that it menaced the latter when it
unjustly suspected it of partiality for Austria. The
English nation is too much judged by the past.
It is not sufficiently chivalrous to engage in a
war of principles, but it would be wrong to suppose it indifferent to justice and humanity in
international questions. Regard for right, and
the spirit of the age, have made great progress
in that nation. In Germany they talk of right;
in England they believe in it—many at least do
so, although English prejudices and English interests, more or less rightly understood, may
occasionally mar the effect of that belief.*

* "Public opinion in England is very favourable to
us at this moment, and this opinion is so formidable
among statesmen at the head of affairs here, that an
armed intervention against us appears not only impolitic
but impossible."—(Zanardini to Manin, 21st of April.)

On the 9th of May, Mr. Cobden wrote to Manin, that
he was certain that the English ministry would not
place itself in opposition to public sentiment, and sua-

This matter is important and little known :

tain the interests of Austria against Italy, either by arms or by diplomacy.   We find in a work very highly esteemed, as well as very favourable to the Italian cause, *Two Years of Revolution in Italy*, by F. T. Perrens, 1857, p. 300, the following passage, which sums up, with regard to Venice, the arguments of the pacific system which found currency in France.

" Bound by the treaties of 1815, France fully maintains the right of the people to violate them as to their internal constitution, as it has done itself; but it cannot assist others without causing an European war, in which it would have England for a foe, who has been a strict observer of those treaties by which she has profited so much; with Russia ready to interfere to defend a principle, and Austria resolved to retain its richest provinces at any price."

Were this picture of Europe in 1848 correct, it might be answered that the Revolution of February had its principal motive in the foreign policy of Louis Philippe, and that revolutions must not be made without at the same time deciding to sustain them at any price. We may repeat a saying of the unfortunate Duke of Orleans, when he felt himself smothered under his father's policy—" It is better to fall upon the Rhine than in the kennels of Paris ;" an excellent maxim for not falling upon the Rhine or anywhere else.   But the picture is not correct, and the armed coalition of England and the Holy Alliance to crush France upon

and a few precise details, as to facts and dates,
are necessary to support our assertions.

On the 2nd of April, Lord Ponsonby, English
Ambassador to Austria, wrote to Lord Palmer-

the occasion of the war in Italy was a chimera. What
we say of England can be proved by facts. As to Russia,
who, it was said, was going to make a war of principles
against France—this Russia of the Holy Alliance and
legitimacy, which for a long time frightened the East,
existed only in appearance. The true Russia—behold it
in what follows. After his noisy demonstrations in the
early days of the Revolution of February, the Emperor
Nicholas assumed an attitude of reserve—then he made
known to the French Government, by the Russian representatives at Naples and London, Messieurs Creptowich
and Brunow, that he was not opposed to liberal and democratic reforms in Italy, provided the territorial arrangements of 1815 were respected—then throwing off
the mask, and putting aside the treaties of 1815, he
intimated that he was ready to offer a *carte blanche*
to the French Republic in the West—that is to say,
Italy independent, and the left bank of the Rhine
for France, provided it gave him a *carte blanche* in the
East. This offer was made at Naples, by M. de Creptowich, the Russian Ambassador, to M. de Raineval, the
French Ambassador. General Cavaignac disregarded
it. It was only upon this that Russia so loudly declared itself the protector of Austria and the treaties:
France was then well assured that she would never have
against her at the same time both Russia and England.

ston that he had received at Vienna news of the Piedmontese invasion. One of the leaders of the revolutionary party at Vienna came to ask of the English ambassador that England should endeavour to obtain an armistice in Italy, so as to secure a peace based upon a pecuniary indemnity for the evacuation of the territory.

M. de Lacour, *chargé d'affaires* from France to Vienna, informed Lord Ponsonby that his government had instructed him to come to an understanding with his lordship, in order to unite the French and English policy as closely as possible. M. de Lacour also spoke to Lord Ponsonby of the project of an arrangement by means of a pecuniary indemnity.

M. de Fiquelmont, Austrian Minister of Foreign Affairs, referred to the treaties of 1815, and asked if England approved of the conduct of Charles Albert and of Lombardy. Lord Ponsonby replied that the British Government had nothing to do with the conduct of the King of Sardinia, but that he could not say that his government would be disposed to employ coercive measures in order to compel the King of Sardinia to desist from his enterprise. M. De Fi-

quelmont requested that the English agents in
Italy should, at least, be instructed not to
exhibit a hostile spirit against Austria.

On the 5th of April, Lord Ponsonby wrote
to Lord Palmerston that M. de Fiquelmont had
informed him that a mission had been given to
Count Hartig, to come to some arrangement in
Italy, if possible.   But the conditions were not
named.   On the 15th of April, Count Dietrichstein, Austrian Ambassador at London, wrote
to Lord Palmerston that the proposed reconciliation was " on the largest basis resulting from
the new political system adopted by Austria."
No further explanation was given; but evidently a constitution was to be offered to Lombardy.   Count Dietrichstein demanded the
conciliatory influence of England to obtain,
above all things, a suspension of arms.

On the 17th of April, Lord Palmerston wrote
to Sir R. Abercromby, at Turin, to urge strongly
upon the Sardinian Government a suspension
of hostilities, and to recommend to Lombardy
to take into consideration the proposals Count
Hartig was charged to offer to it.

Lord Palmerston did not reply to Lord Ponsonby's letter of the 5th until the 20th.   He instructed him to say that the British Government had advised the King of Sardinia to observe a strict neutrality towards France and Austria: this advice had not been followed: it was for Austria now to determine her own course; but M. de Fiquelmont was entirely mistaken as to the state of things in Italy (in wishing to propose an Austro-Italian constitution), and as to a pecuniary arrangement, it would, no doubt, be advantageous to Austria, but it was doubtful if the time for it was yet come.

Thus, on the 20th of April, Lord Palmerston, so far from believing that the Italian provinces would accept a reconciliation with the empire, even doubted if Austria could obtain an indemnity from them.

On the 24th of April, Lord Normanby, the English Minister at Paris, communicated to Lord Palmerston an important conversation with M. de Lamartine: the latter had said that it was probable Charles Albert would be beaten; and that such an event would greatly complicate the position of the French Government: that there would be a great cry in France that they should

come to the assistance of the Italians. He wished
to do nothing without the consent of England.
He had always thought that the affairs of the peninsula could never be arranged, except by a conference or a congress. His wish was that whenever
this took place, England and France should come
to an understanding on the subject.

On the 27th of April, Sir R. Abercromby
communicated his instructions to the Marquis
Pareto, the Sardinian Minister of Foreign Affairs,
who enquired of him if he knew the nature of
·the propositions that Count Hartig was em-
powered to make. Sir R. Abercromby replied
that he was entirely without information on that
subject. The council of Ministers of the King
of Sardinia despatched its president, Count
Cæsar Balbo, from Turin to the camp of Charles
Albert, to obtain the king's approval of the resolution which the ministers had taken to reject
the armistice, until the enemy made his propositions known, and replied, through M. Pareto, to
the English Ambassador in the following terms:—

" We do not think we can honourably enter
into negociations with regard to Lombardy and
Venetia, until the object for which we entered these
provinces is attained:" that is as it was said in

the message of Charles Albert to the provisional government of Milan.   " When there will no longer be an Austrian on the soil of Italy." (30th of April.)

Lord Palmerston was already informed of this reply, before even the parleyings at Turin, on the 19th of April.   Count Hartig, in place of offering conditions of peace, had simply published a proclamation to the Lombardo-Venetian people, inviting them to return to their allegiance to their legitimate sovereign.   Lord Palmerston, informed of this strange proceeding of the Austrians, wrote to Lord Ponsonby, on the 3rd of May, that under such circumstances the refusal of an armistice by the King of Sardinia was justified.

On the same day (3rd of May), ·Lord Normanby wrote to Lord Palmerston, that he had seen M. de Lamartine.   " I alluded to the question of French intervention in Italy.   I asked him if it were not true that Count Fiquelmont had communicated to him, through Count d'Appony, his intention of entering into negociations respecting Lombardy.   M. de Lamartine acknowledged that he had, and explained to me how this communication had been made to him."

On the previous day (2nd of May), the Venetian envoy, Zanardini, after a conversation with M. de Lamartine, left in a state of consternation. The French Minister had said that it was his belief that Charles Albert was betraying the Italian cause; that Austria, from what he had learned from Count d'Appony, had given up Milan; but that it would sacrifice its last soldier, and its last coin, rather than give up Venice. "I consider Venice," he added, "as lost to you! ... We are too poor to make war."*

Some days afterwards (6th of May), M. de

* Zanardini to Manin, 4th of May. Austria was still poorer :—As to the last soldier and the last coin, it is not every one will spend them. It might have been very well for the France of 1792. There must be for this the desperate enthusiasm of a nation fighting for its existence. Reasons of state will not suffice, nor yet those still less heroic interests of which the Augsburg Gazette has just published this characteristic display. "A meeting of the richest bankers earnestly begged the Viennese Government never to abandon the Italian provinces. As to the manufacturers of Austria and Bohemia, the idea of losing Venetia and Lombardy *as markets*, threw them into a state of consternation." (A. de la Forge.)

Lamartine confessed to the Venetian agents, that considerations connected with his foreign policy would not allow him to consent that the muskets they asked for—the money for which was ready —should be sent direct to Venice.

The Venetian agents, imagining they could see a compact concluded between Austria, England, the Provisional government of France, and Piedmont, to sacrifice Venice, entreated their government, in their despatches, to send to Paris an official representative on a mission, to demand publicly the recognition of the Venetian Republic.   " If the French Government," they said, " will not, the Assembly will." Venice would then have been under the protection of the French nation.

What, then, was the real intention of M. de Lamartine, and what were the verbal overtures which Count d'Appony made to him—overtures which are not explained in Lord Normanby's despatches?

M. de Lamartine informs us in his *History of the Revolution of* 1848, that " the envoys of Austria submitted to his judgment the offers the cabinet of the Emperor was disposed to make to

Sardinia.   The question related to the surrender
of Lombardy and the duchies of Parma and
Modena, and the grant of a constitution to
Venice, under the independent viceroyalty of a
prince of the house of Austria.*

  M. de Lamartine did not hesitate to acknowledge that these propositions to a great extent satisfied the legitimate ambition of emancipation in
Italy, and he encouraged the Austrian cabinet to
carry on negotiations on these bases. Twice these
overtures were made semi-officially, and twice he
held the same language. He would have been neither statesman nor patriot if he had rejected them,
for the adoption of such an arrangement would
have permitted France to rectify one of her frontiers impaired after the Hundred Days. . . . .†

  * According to the recollections of M. de Lamartine,
Count d'Appony must have gone further even than the
independent viceroyalty ; that is to say one responsible
to the Emperor alone, and not to the cabinet of Vienna :
he must have spoken of making Venetia a second Tuscany, under an Austrian prince, independent of the empire, and, doubtless, only allied to it. Count d'Appony
went further in his proposals in words than by writing,
because it would be easier to disavow the former..

  † From the beginning of May to the beginning of
June

Thus, the conclusion of the Revolution of Italy was to be—Lombardy united to Piedmont, Savoy united to France, and Venice, not to be unconditionally left to herself, but finally given up to Austria;—*tied* to Austria !

We repeat it with profound regret, but it is our duty to repeat it, this policy was incompatible with international principles, and with the policy of the Revolution : even before the Revolution, it must be admitted, that none of the statesmen of the old French school, from Henry IV. and Richelieu to Chauvelin and d'Argenson, had supported the idea of leaving Venice and Verona to Austria.   France could neither exercise nor permit foreign dominion in Italy.

This policy, we repeat, was the error of a great mind, not the weakness of a timid heart.*

* This policy is systematized in an article in *la Bien public,* of the 14th of August, 1848, where the plan of the negociation M. Lamartine proposed to sustain in an European congress, which he wished to convoke at Berne, is given. It was declared that Venice ought to make the balance of Italian independence, and be *neutralized* under the administration of an Archduke.   M. de Lamartine did not wish to leave Venice and Verona to Austria, purely and simply : but they might reckon

While Lord Palmerston, receiving no communication from Austria, wrote to Lord Ponsonby, to invite the Austrian Government to take into its serious consideration whether it would not be more to its interests to treat with Lombardy,* than to reckon upon a doubtful military success, and drawing the French against its arms (8th May).

At Paris, the Provisional Government, transformed into an executive commission by the constitutional assembly, held council on the affairs of Italy; and there could be little doubt that immediate intervention would be decided upon, without taking into account the refusal of Piedmont and Lombardy. It was at least fully resolved, upon the proposal of M. de Lamartine himself, to declare boldly to the assembly, the intention of crossing the Alps upon the first appeal (12th May).

that, if they left Austria a footing under any title whatever, it would employ it to reconquer its full past dominion at any price.

* Did Lord Palmerston understand by Lombardy, Milan or Lombardo-Venetia? We are convinced that it was the latter. And we shall soon see why.

There was no contradiction in M. de Lamartine. The non-official overtures of Count d'Appony could only be a decoy; and a victory over Charles Albert would have caused Austria to retract its offers. M. de Lamartine wished to treat securely for Savoy, and proportionably protect Milan.

. On the 13th of May, a demonstration in an opposite direction to the secret deliberation of the executive commission, took place in the Chamber of Deputies of Piedmont. The Minister Pareto replied to the questions of a representative, that the French would not come till they were sent for; and as they had not been asked, they had not come!

Questions were also put in the National Assembly at Paris. The uneasiness of the Venetian and Milanese agents had transpired; and M. de Lamartine, in the name of the government, protested from the tribune against any suspicion of an understanding with Austria; and declared that, if the French army had not entered Italy, it was because the Italians had not wished it (23rd May).

In England, also, public sentiment was fa-

vourable to Italy; and Lord Palmerston immediately after gave the same assurances to Par-
liament that M. de Lamartine had given to the
Constituent Assembly.

A few days after the sitting of the Constituent Assembly, two envoys, M. M. Aleardi and
Gar, sent by Venice to the French Republic,
arrived at Paris. According to Manin's instructions, they were to claim the formal recognition of the Venetian Republic, and to entreat
France to promise to the people, and formally
notify to sovereign rulers, that it would never
again suffer, beyond the Alps, a new treaty of
Campo Formio, and a new partition of Poland.*

* Diplomatic instructions to M. M. Aleardi and Gar, of
the 15th of May : MS. We remark the following passage : " It is needless to recommend you to take no part
in any meeting where men, even the most honourable,
conspire against any European sovereign : conspire yourselves, but do so openly ; conspire with the most eminent Germans that you may meet in Paris ; so that true
Germany may at last understand that, if it wishes Austria to
become German, it must destroy the Austrian monarchy."
Manin, in the same instructions, recommended the
envoys to exert themselves energetically with the French
press and its principal representative. On the 5th of June,

The envoys presented themselves to M. Bastide,* the new Minister for Foreign Affairs,
who protested his sympathy with the Venetjan
government, but added " his regret at not being
able at that moment, to officially recognise this ,
government." †　Thus, the new minister, whose

he wrote in this style, a letter, developing to a French
constituent, who the preceding year had travelled in
Italy, and published a very violent book against Austria
—M. de Cormenin. He declared himself, in the present
condition of Italy, for a federation of States of nearly
equal strength ; a combination which he knew would be
more agreeable to the French republicans than a kingdom of Italy.

* The ministerial functions had been separated from
those of the Executive commission at which M. de Lamartine sat, and which was a kind of Directory.

† Aleardi and Gar to Manin, 2nd of June.　On this
subject we find the following passage, in the notes of
the consul, M. Vasseur.　He describes his first interview with Manin :—" His countenance assumed an
aspect of sadness, when, having enquired of me what
would be the superscription of the letters addressed
to me by our minister, I replied,—*A M. le Consul de
France, a Venice* (at Venice, and not the Republic of
Venice).　Our dissensions," said he (the dissensions
relative to the Republic or the fusion with Piedmont),
" would disappear, if France would recognise our young

character and sentiments are warmly praised in the envoys' despatches, had also to submit to the consequences of the negative impulse previously given to the ministry, in what concerned Venice.

During these incidents at Paris, Austria officially renewed with Lord Palmerston the overtures it had officially made to M. de Lamartine. On the 12th of May, M. de Fiquelmont announced to Lord Ponsonby, that the Austrian cabinet had sent Baron Hummelauër to London, charged with two plans of arrangement with Italy: the second to be presented to the English cabinet only, if it refused its intervention in favour of the first.

On the 23rd of May, Baron Hummelauër, Austrian Envoy Extraordinary at London, by virtue of his instructions, requested English mediation, and proposed the administrative separation of the Lombardo-Venetian kingdom from the government of Vienna, and its neutralization. Lord Palmerston replied, "It is too late !"

Republic. It would give us a moral strength which we do not now possess ; but I see that our hopes are vain !"

On the 24th of May, Baron Hummelauër presented the second proposal; which was, to abandon Lombardy : Venetia remaining under the vice-royalty of an Archduke, but with separate and national administration, representation, finances, and army. This proposal M. de Lamartine was said to approve; only he had not foreseen that the Austrian envoy requested the good offices of England to obtain from Piedmont a defensive alliance with Austria against France.

Lord Palmerston, for the second time, replied, "It is too late! It raises," he said, "well-founded doubts upon the real utility to Austria of recovering the whole of its Italian provinces. The spirit of nationality has become so strong and universal among the Italians, that to keep these provinces in subjection, will compel Austria to a display of power, and to expenses, which can hardly compensate for their possession. As to maintaining the Venetian provinces under the authority of the Emperor, Her Britannic Majesty's government fears that matters have gone too far for such an arrangement to have the slightest chance of being accepted by the Venetians. Consequently, Her Majesty's government would not wish a proposal to be made which it knows beforehand will be positively refused by one of the parties."

Lord Palmerston concluded by saying, that the English government would interpose only if Austria included in its propositions such portion of the Venetian territory as might be arranged between the interested parties; and by this portion, it understood not only Venice, and the greater part of Venetia, but also the Italian Tyrol: and it explained this by saying, for example, that the frontier between Venice and Trieste might be on the Tagliamento, and on the north between Trento and Bolzano (3rd of June).

On the 9th of June, Lord Ponsonby reported to Lord Palmerston a conference he had had at Innspruck with the Archduke John, then at the head of the Austrian government; who claimed absolutely, the Adige and Verona, and consequently held to the Hummelauër proposition.

The Austrian cabinet, losing all hope of being supported by England, again turned to the French government. According to a letter from the Austrian minister, Wessenberg, to M. de Dietrichstein (16th of June), the French government had applied to Austria, through the organ of its *chargé d'affaires* at Vienna, M. de La Cour. Lord Ponsonby, on his part, wrote to Lord Palmerston, that Baron Wessenberg had announced to him the sending of an envoy to Paris with a declaration, authorising the French cabinet to make known officially, that Austria had resolved to agree to the absolute independence of the Milanese: that is to say,—that the proposition made and rejected at London, was renewed at Paris. " The baron appeared to me well satisfied with making an official declaration exactly in the sense desired by M. de La Cour. . . . He assured me, that if Venetia remained united to Austria, it would give to her an extremely liberal constitution (12th of June)."

We quote without commentary, having no means of examining the despatches of M. de La Cour.

On the 13th of June, Baron Wessenberg wrote to Count Casati, president of the provisional government of Milan, that he should offer peace, based on the independence of Lombardy. Orders were at the same time sent to Radetzky, to propose an armistice to Charles Albert.

The Lombard provisional government replied that it would enter into negociations with Austria only upon its substituting for the recognition of the independence of Lombardy, that of the independence of all the Venetian provinces (18th of June). A reply the more noble, inasmuch as Vicenza was lost, and Venetia was failing at the time!

Charles Albert again refused the armistice.

On the 20th of June, Lord Palmerston, in a despatch to Lord Ponsonby, maintained his offer of mediation on the basis he had established on the 3rd of June (Venetian independence), and his opinion as to the impossibility of Austria keeping the line of the Adige. He believed, that if the war continued, the Austrians would be driven out of the whole of Italy without indemnity; "the population being utterly hostile to them."*

* The English Ambassador at Turin, Hon. R. Abercromby, was of the same opinion. See his letter of the 2nd of July, in which he so energetically expressed him-

While Lombardy and Piedmont rejected the overtures of Austria, Manin sent word to his agents at Paris that Venice could not invite the French army before consulting with the other Italian states, and earnestly begging that France would act upon Austria, " by words, half advice and half threats," and also put the question to Charles Albert if he still thought that Italy would suffice for herself.*   (16th of June.)

On the very day that Manin wrote this letter, the Executive Commission, at Paris, was deliberating upon the affairs of Italy.   After two days of debating, it was decided that intervention could

self against the pretensions of Austria to keep Venetia, and in favour of an Italian kingdom.

* Manin to Aleardi and Gar.   The following passage may be quoted :—" The principal danger of French intervention will be that the war may become social, that is to say, a war between those who have something to lose and those who have nothing, and in that case it would be more fearful than the Revolution of the past century; for there principles governed the passions, while here passions, and those the least noble, will silence principles. . . . . . To escape the evils pointed out, we must arrange with Frenchmen, most respected for their probity, so that, if war must take place, it will be they who shall give it its rallying cry."

no longer be deferred; that the French army must cross the Alps without waiting for the approbation of Charles Albert; that the government would afterwards lay before the Assembly the great questions relative to the direction of the intervention; lastly, that three hundred battalions of *gardes mobiles* must be immediately organized.* The decree respecting the three hundred battalions appeared in the *Moniteur* of the 17th of June.

Such, from the 16th to the 23rd of June, was the position of Venice, which, a few days before, believed herself lost and deserted by England and France. England treated the independence of Venice as a settled question, it only admitted discussions as to its frontier. France was actually moving her troops.

What would France have done beyond the Alps? In the report of the Minister of the Interior respecting the *gardes mobiles*, an idea adverse to Venice suggested a phrase which indicated that the aim of the armament was the union of Savoy with France, rather than the entire emancipation

---

* We rely on the testimony of an auricular witness for the account of these two secret sittings.

of Italy ; but nothing of the kind seems to have been discussed in the Executive Commission nor in the councils of the Ministry.* The question would have come fresh before the Constituent

* This is the language of the report :—" The Executive Commission firmly cherishes the hope of maintaining
peace. Still France will not assist without anticipating
some re-arrangement of territory. She cannot tolerate
an increase of power in her neighbours to the weakening
of its own power, without compensating herself."

The *Bien Public*, of the 20th of June, a journal under
the editorial influence of M. de Lamartine, commented
on the decree of mobilization in the following terms :
" The Republic will not permit the King of Piedmont to
extend his grasp from one sea of Italy to the other : to
acquire twelve millions more subjects, four fortresses,
Alexandria, Peschiera, Mantua, and Verona, and re-create
for his own benefit a sovereignty like that of Austria
over the Peninsula.

" Evidently the French Republic must watch narrowly
this absorption of Lombardy by Piedmont. It must
claim guarantee, indemnity, compensation for this new
extension of territory and this accumulation of power
which the King of Sardinia might bring from Lombardy
against our frontier. We cannot allow, at only a few
steps from Lyons and Toulon, at our very gates, on our
flanks, a State to raise, by increase in its population,
the figure of its army from one hundred thousand soldiers to two hundred thousand."

Assembly; and beyond all doubt, in the full
light of day, the policy of arranging with Austria
would have vanished.   The majority of the
government would have pronounced against the
direction of foreign affairs, if the latter had not
been voluntarily changed.   The Assembly, before
the gaze of France and Europe, would assuredly
have voted for the complete enfranchisement of all
Italy as well as of Venice; and no authority, no
eloquence could have stopped the logic of sentiments and facts.

It was too late! . . . . . Some weeks before,
foreign war would, doubtless, have saved France
from civil war!   Before the country could learn
the resolution of the government, the passions
exasperated by four months of social crisis, broke
out.   On the 23rd of June, Paris, seized with a
horrible delirium, tore out its vitals with its own
hands.   The Executive Commission was wrecked
in the storm, and mutilated France let fall the
sword it had stained with its own blood!

Europe, and especially Italy, had not to wait
long for the consequences of these dreadful days.*

* See as to the course of English diplomacy discussed
in this chapter, the note at the commencement of the
second volume.

CHAPTER VI.

Question of Fusion with Piedmont—The Provinces declare for Fusion—Views of Manin on this subject—
The Venetian Civic Guard ask for French Intervention—The Italian Governments oppose it—Assembly
of the Province of Venice—Sitting of the 4th of July
—Manin accepts the Fusion and quits office.

WE now return to Venice, and see what she did
for herself, while her destiny was debated elsewhere without her, and while great and sinister
distant events so fatally compromised her cause.

In her internal policy as in her diplomacy,
there was, in fact, but one question—to avoid a
Campo Formio at any cost. The best means—
were they to maintain the Republic, or to unite
with Lombardy and Piedmont under the constitutional sceptre of Charles Albert?

Venice, with its immediate dependencies, had
a great republican majority.   In the provinces,
the sentiment of national unity increased, and
was strengthened by a little jealousy against the
ancient dominion of the Queen of the Lagoons,
but especially by the instinct of danger which led
her to concentrate herself through the feeling of
the inevitable military weakness of the Venetian
government, and the fear that the King of Sardinia would show but little zeal for aiding a
republic—these made the partizans of the *fusion*
more and more numerous.   Since the 20th of
April, Vicenza had directly solicited Piedmontese
aid ; on the 29th of April, the deputies of
Padua, Vicenza, Treviso, Rovigo, and Belluno,
in an address to the Lombard government, had
expressed a wish for the union of Venetia with
Lombardy ; they had communicated this address
to the Minister of War of Piedmont.   Manin
and his colleagues, opposed to a kingdom of
Upper Italy, were, on the contrary, favourable
to the formation of a Lombardo-Venetian republic, sustained abroad by the French republic.
Resolved, under any circumstances, to submit to
the national will, their first thought, as is shown

in the instructions given to the Minister Paleocapa, on the 21st of April, was to reserve the
solution of everything to the Venetian Constituent Assembly; then, in compliance with the
wishes of the provinces, they made another step;
they assented to the proposal of the Lombard provisional government to assemble a single constituent assembly for Lombardy and Venetia, to
regulate the political conditions of the country
after victory. This decision was published at
Venice on the 12th of May.

The Lombard government was not faithful to
its agreement. Under the impression of the
declaration of Charles Albert, that he would negociate only after entirely freeing the Italian soil,
the government of Milan gave direction the same
day (12th of May), for the opening, in all the
Lombard communes, of registers for voting
for and against fusion with Piedmont. The
provinces of Padua, Vicenza, Treviso, and Rovigo followed the example of Lombardy without
the permission of the Venetian government. On
the 31st of May, their delegates presented to
this government a declaration, which was both
an apology the provincial committees felt them-

selves obliged to make, and a summons for Venice to imitate them. It intimated that, if by the 4th of June they received no reply, however deeply afflicted they might be at separating themselves from Venice, the representatives of the four provincial committees would set out for Milan, in order to regulate with the Lombards the *régime* to be established during the transition, between the vote for fusion and the meeting of the Constituent Assembly. This Constituent Assembly was to determine not the question of fusion, but only its conditions. The Venetian government replied, on the 2d of June, that it would consult the wishes of the people, by means of an assembly of the province of Venice, convoked for the 18th; meanwhile, it authorized its representative at Milan to participate in the deliberations of the mixed commission which had been announced to it.

This was moderation, assuredly, and more conciliatory forms could not be employed; but in being moderate, Manin and his friends were not giving up their own opinions. They did not intend to give way without legal resistance, nor without deep and solemn discussion. To judge equitably of the policy of Manin, it is necessary

thoroughly to understand the motives of the opposition he made in 1848 to this same fusion,
which he supported some years later, under circumstances entirely different. Republican in
sentiment and principle, but patriot before republican, he would not have hesitated on the first
any more than he did on the second occasion, to
sacrifice his feelings to the interests of Italy—but
he did not admit that it was the interest of Italy
then. Politic and practical, before everything,
he regarded the present only as the starting
point for the future. Now, what was the present of Italy in the spring of 1848? Whatever might be the secret sentiments of princes,
the leading fact was the coalition of the different
Italian States against foreign dominion. Was it
then necessary to give to any one of these princes
an overwhelming preponderance over the others,
by the constitution of a kingdom of Upper Italy;
and thus furnish them with a reason, if they were
sincere, or a pretext, if they were not, for abandoning the common cause?* Would it not have

* Venice wished to accede to Unity, or to a Federation, but not to a State which did not comprehend *the
whole of Italy*, and which would have been too great
to enter conveniently into a federation.

been better to recognise in Pius IX. a kind of honorary supremacy or Italian presidency which would disturb no one?   With one or more republics in Upper Italy, would they not be much better assured of the support of France, to which they must doubtless have recourse at last, and which felt hurt by the independent and almost hostile attitude of Charles Albert?   If the King of Sardinia had possessed the strength and capacity to sustain the bold part to which he aspired, if it had chanced that his genius and success had made of him, not a Duke of Milan, but a King of Italy, then every other consideration should give way: but Manin was persuaded to the contrary.

Such were Manin's ideas during the early days of the Revolution.   Grave events subsequently modified the situation.   The counter-revolution had succeeded at Naples.   Manin had divested his mind of every illusion as to the co-operation of Pius IX., although the Venetian Government continued officially to invoke the name of the Holy Father. It was not the fear of alienating the other princes that deterred the liberator of Venice from accepting Charles Albert, but a more poignant

fear. If Venice declined to govern and defend
itself, if it placed itself in the hands of the
Piedmontese commanders and administrators,
what reverses might not happen! Charles Albert,
to retain Milan, might renounce Venice by a
new treaty of Campo Formio, and the noble city
be disarmed and sold, as in 1797.

The convocation of an assembly for the 18th
of June, to decide the question of fusion, strongly
agitated Venice. The civic guard and the people
made earnest manifestations in favour of a republic (4th of June). But the demonstrations
on the Square of St. Mark ceased immediately
the gondoliers and the fishermen knew that
these tumultuous movements displeased him
whom they so well styled *their Manin.*

Meanwhile Vicenza succumbed. The Neapolitan squadron, after the reiterated orders of its
king, at length set sail; and General Pepe
entered Venice with the two thousand patriots
who had scorned those odious commands. (10—
13 June).

Venice cried aloud : in four and twenty hours
the civic guard unanimously signed a request to
have recourse to French arms. (12—13 June).

The Venetian Government prorogued until the
3rd of July the Assembly that ought to have
assembled on the 18th of June to decide upon
the fusion; it gave the command of the little
Venetian army to General Pepe, and, by a
touching appeal, invited all the cities of Italy
to assist Venice with arms and money: while,
by despatches to all the Italian Governments,
the King of Naples only excepted, clearly put
the ominous *fara da sè* into a state of doubt.

In the despatch sent to the Piedmontese
Government, the Venetian Government alluded
to a "sinister rumour" which terrified Venice:
the rumour of an act "so abominable and impossible, that it would be a crime to admit the
supposition"—that is to say, a renewal of Campo
Formio. It referred to the deeds and promises
of the King of Sardinia, demanded, in the name
of the Venetian people, what means had been
adopted by that prince to assure their safety,
and protested that if Charles Albert again affirmed, solemnly, that Italy would suffice for
herself, Italy and Venice would take him at his
word. Under delicate and respectful forms, this
was putting the King of Sardinia into the di-

lemma of renewing, at the cost of a fearful responsibility, an affirmation that events became every day more hazardous, or of renouncing his anti-French policy.   (13th of June.)

In the circular addressed to the cabinets of Rome, Tuscany, and Sicily,* the Venetian Government was more explicit.

" We appeal to the Italian people as arbitrators of our destinies. . . . And we enquire of each of their governments if they believe it possible that Italy now suffices for herself?   Many of the people of Venetia urge our government to call in foreign aid on honourable conditions. But we, who do not wish to decide, from this corner of Italy, a question which concerns the common country, we ask each of the States of the Peninsula to give a clear and prompt reply." (14th of June.)

Piedmont did not reply.   Charles Albert dared not utter the words required of him, nor wished to recognize the necessity of an appeal to France. The Tuscan Government was divided and weak.   Corsini, the Minister of Foreign

* Sicily continued separated from Naples, and at war with Ferdinand.

Affairs, contrary to the opinion of the Prime Minister Ridolfi,* sided with the Grand Duke, and rejected the proposal to appeal to the *stranger*—at least until the irreparable disasters of the Italian army had rendered this succour indispensable. (18th June.) The Roman and Sicilian Governments also replied in the negative. (21st of June.)† The latter, which thought of calling the second son of Charles Albert to the throne, was under Piedmontese influence. The monarchical and constitutional parties, through fear of the republic and of Socialism, and the Mazzinian Republican party, were all agreed upon rejecting the sole chance of safety for Italy.‡

Manin reluctantly gave way before this kind of infatuation, and deferred all decisive steps as to France.

The silence the Venetian government held

* The Marquis Ridolfi resigned a few days afterwards, on this very question of French intervention.

† The Pope sent his benediction to Venice: this was a poor compensation for a French army!

‡ It was not only at Venice that the people's good sense protested against this blindness of parties. In the early part of July, there was at Milan a strong expression of opinion in favour of French intervention.

unwillingly, on the petition of the civic guard, began to excite in this body, that is to say in the Venetian citizens, a reaction in the Piedmontese direction.   As they would not call upon the French, Charles Albert must decide, at any risk, to make a last effort in favour of Venice : such was the specious argument successfully put forth by the fusionist party.   The fall of the renowned fortress of Palma Nuova, the resistance of which had previously rendered the occupation of Frioul by the Austrians precarious (27th of June), renewed the emotions of the fall of Vicenza, and caused a panic in Venice.   The government, knowing that a tumultuous demonstration in favour of Piedmont was preparing in the ranks of the civic guard, countermanded a review appointed to take place on the 29th of June.   The staff of the civic guard disobeyed : the review took place amid many shouts for Charles Albert, and a few outcries against Manin and Tommaseo, excited by the latter having sent, as if in defiance of the civic guard, some troops of the line to share the posts with them.   The staff proceeded to the government palace, and informed the president that he had caused an imposing manifestation in favour of fusion.

"What does the civic guard understand it has done by that?" enquired Manin.

"It understands that it has voted for fusion."

"That shall be taken into consideration: but I cannot neglect this opportunity of observing how much it is to be regretted, that while the lower classes of the people allow themselves to be persuaded to await calmly and respectfully the coming vote of the assembly, the noble corps of the civic guard gives so bad an example, in illegally anticipating that vote; thereby perilling public tranquillity, while the very object of its institution is to maintain it."

Manin immediately hastened to the square of St. Mark, and declared that the order to send troops of the line to the posts held by the civic guard (a very imprudent order, in fact) had not proceeded from him. He was surrounded by the crowd, which redoubled its usual acclamations, as if to justify him. One of the crowd threw himself upon Manin's neck, sobbing, and embraced him.

"I love my country above everything," cried

Manin ; "and I am ready to sacrifice all for her good, even my most cherished convictions."

The people reconducted him to San Pater-nian.

The assembly of the province of Venice (the ancient *Dogado*) met on the 3rd of July, in the hall of the grand council, in the ducal palace. In the morning Manin sent the following note to his wife :—

"I expect that no member of my family will express either approval, disapprobation, or impatience. If you think you will not be able to appear indifferent, keep away from the meeting. I am sure, that at this critical hour you would not wish to add to my misfortunes, that of being disobeyed by my own family."

The first sitting passed in preliminary arrangements. Manin explained the motives, and the threefold objects of the convocation. 1st. To decide if the question relative to their political condition should be discussed now, or after the war. 2nd. To decide, in the event of an immediate discussion, if Venice should remain an independent State, or be incorporated with Piedmont. 3rd. To replace or confirm the

members of the provisional government.   Manin
prevented his friends, as well as his adversaries,
from going beyond the limits assigned to a
wholly special assembly, which was not a constitutional one.   At the commencement of the
sitting of the 4th, in his capacity of minister of
foreign affairs, he made a report upon their
external relations.   With respect to French
ntervention, demanded in numerous petitions,
he said, that the government had wished "previously to question the other governments of
Italy, so that they might declare if really the
Italian forces were sufficient to drive the Austrians out of Italy ; and if they were not, that
they should join with us, and the aid of the
French nation be claimed in behalf of the whole
Italian nation."

Casselli, minister of domestic finance, then
read a very gloomy report on the state of the
exchequer : a partisan of fusion, he did not
attempt to soften its hues.   A magnificent discourse by Tommaseo, in favour of the Republic,
reanimated the assembly, without reviving a
party, formed, not by contrary political opinions,
but by the feeling, ill or well founded, of neces-

sity. Another of the ministers, Paleocapa, replied to Tommaseo, energetically supporting the
fusion. The government was openly divided.
The assembly was divided, as well as the government. There was also a majority for fusion in
the civic guard ; a majority less decided, perhaps, than it was a few days previously ; but no
such majority existed among the mass of the
people.* Had Manin, supported by one half of
the assembly, continued his opposition, either
the reception or the rejection of the fusion by a
small majority would have disorganised Venice.

Manin ascended the tribune, and spoke
thus :—

" I have the same opinion to-day that I had
on the 22nd of March, when, before the gates
of the arsenal, and on the Square of St. Mark,
I proclaimed the Republic. I have it still ; all
had it, then : all do not entertain it now. (*Agitation*.) I desire to speak words of love and
harmony, and I beg not to be interrupted.—It

* The people began to enquire, what advantage would
result from the fusion with Piedmont, as Charles Albert
did not come to their assistance ? (The intermediate
country was held by the Austrians.)

is a fact, that at the present time, all of us do
not hold that opinion : it is also a fact, that the
enemy are at our gates : that this enemy expects
and desires discord in our country—impregnable
while we are in harmony with each other, but
easily overcome if a prey to civil war. As for
myself, I abstain from all discussion upon my
opinions, or upon those held by others. I am
about to demand a great sacrifice. I am
about to demand it of my own party, the generous republican party. Give to the enemy who
is at our gates, who reckons upon our dissensions
—give him a decisive contradiction ! Prove to
him that at this hour we think neither of being
royalists nor republicans ; but that we are Italians ! To the republicans, I say, the future is ours !
Everything done now is provisional ; the decision
belongs to the Italian Diet—to Rome !" *

* *To Rome !* These words prove that the idea of
remaking Rome the capital of New Italy—so far as Italy
can have a capital—that is, the place of meeting for the
Italian national assembly, is not, as has been often repeated, a dream of Mazzini's. It is the almost universal idea among Italian patriots. All the great cities are
jealous of each other : not one is jealous of Rome, nor
will dispute her traditional supremacy. Rome, the
Latin centre, in an emancipated Italy, would produce

Thunders of applause shook this illustrious hall, which had never echoed with nobler sentiments in the palmiest days of ancient Venice. The whole assembly crowded round the seat to which the orator had returned. Everyone sought to embrace and thank him. The minister Castelli rushed to the tribune, and raising his hands to heaven, cried,—

"The country is saved! *Viva Manin!*" which cry was responded to by all present.

A vote was demanded. Manin, in a voice weakened by emotion, asked for a moment's repose. The assembly was strongly agitated. Manin fainted, and was borne out in a state of unconsciousness. The violence of his emotion, the great struggle he had had with himself, accelerated the palpitations of his heart almost to suffocation. It was one of the first symptoms of an affection of the heart, which he had contracted at his daughter's bed of suffering, and which carried him off nine years afterwards.

After the lapse of half an hour Manin returned, and fusion with the Sardinian states,

an equilibrium between the two centres of action in the north and south,—Gallic Milan and Greek Naples.

"upon the same conditions as Lombardy," was almost unanimously voted.[*]

Next day, upon the proposal of a deputy, who asked the assembly to declare that Manin had deserved well of his country, Manin spoke as follows :—

"If my fellow citizens wish to shew themselves grateful for a very simple act, I beg and pray of them to let the harmony that was inaugurated in this place yesterday, continue so long as the enemy remains in Italy ! I say no more. For the love of God, say no more about parties, so long as the enemy is not driven out ! We can talk afterwards. We must speak together now as brothers ! This is the only recompense I ask of you !"

The vote for the election of the new members of the new provisional government was passed. Manin was re-elected by a large majority.

* "Obeying the supreme necessity for delivering all Italy from the yoke of the foreigner, and with the view of pursuing the war of independence with the greatest possible efficacy . . . . . we vote . . . . . etc." *Raccolta,* vol. ii., p. 484.

Manin warmly expressed his gratitude to the assembly, but would not accept his election. " I was, I am, and I shall remain, a Republican. I can be nothing under a monarchy. I may be in the opposition, but not in the government. I have made a sacrifice, but not denied a principle. Besides, I am exhausted by the fatigues, and even by the pleasures of the last three months. I can do no more ; my head will not bear it."

Every means of persuasion were resorted to, but in vain ; and the assembly had to elect the new government from among the deputies, who had sustained the cause of fusion.

CHAPTER VII.

Defeat of Charles Albert—The Piedmontese Commissioners take possession of Venice—Fall of Milan and
Armistice of Salasco—The eleventh of August—Rising
of Venice—*Governero io*—Manin becomes Dictator.

MANIN, descending from his throne, retired
holding himself in an attitude of observation
and of expectancy. As in the days of his captivity, events imposed on him a halt, a necessary
repose, in order to re-establish, for the second
time, his impaired strength, and to prepare him
for the efforts of a longer and more heroic
struggle. The fusion (as Manin and Tommaseo
had fully predicted) remedied neither the dangers
of war nor the distress in the finances. A small
sum of money and a handful of soldiers, sent by
Charles Albert, testified to his good will, but

also to his weakness.   The Austrian corps of observation grew bolder, and commenced to push forward vigorously.   Bold sorties, which ruined their works, and left open the approaches to the fort of Malghera, the great advanced defence of Venice, showed what might be hoped from the little army formed under Manin (6th to 9th July).

The enemy was really not in a position to assault Venice until the fate of the campaign between Radetsky and Charles Albert was decided.   The position of the King of Sardinia became more and more perilous.   He had rejected the elements and tactics of the revolutionary war, and the elements and tactics of regular war began to fail him ; soldiers could not be made of the Lombard recruits in less than three months ; the Piedmontese reserves were little else than recruits ; and the solid nucleus of his army was now notoriously inferior in numbers to the reinforced Austrians.   In this condition of things concentration was indispensable.   Instead of this, Charles Albert, while continuing to blockade Mantua, of taking which he could have no serious expectation, remained deployed from Rivoli to Man-

tua and beyond.   He felt himself in great peril,
but did nothing to remove himself out of it, and
his heart was full of anguish.   Of all external
remedies, one alone could prove efficacious—an
appeal to France; and Charles Albert preferred
going headlong to ruin rather than make it.*
It must be admitted, however, that the direction
of foreign affairs in France would seem to excuse
him.   It did not show itself so friendly as to

* From the discussion between Count Cavour and
M. Bastide (*vide Le Siècle* of 8th May, 1858), it appears
that in the course of July, French intervention was
offered for the last time to Charles Albert; but after
what had preceded and what followed, we may believe
that this intervention, in pursuance of that prepared by
M. Lamartine, would have had for its object, not the
driving out the Austrians by force of arms from the
whole of Italy, but the negociating beyond the Alps
rather than on this side of it.   Nevertheless, it was a
great misfortune that the entry of the French into Italy
did not take place.   It would have prevented the reverses of the Piedmontese and the fall of Milan; the
energetic protest which would have burst from Venice
against every project of treaty leaving Austria any authority whatever over Venetia; and the good feeling of the
English cabinet for Venice would have undoubtedly
controlled and strengthened the policy of the French
government.

warrant his giving up his fears. And on the one hand he wished to renew the league with the other Italian princes, which he had evaded in April, and which, in July, the Pope and the King of Naples had in their turn rejected. On the other hand, he exhibited more embarrassment than pleasure when the deputies of the Venetian provinces came to present him the act of fusion. He had not the power to defend these provinces which gave themselves to him, and he did not feel himself in a condition to abandon them. He sent the deputies to his ministers; and instead of replying directly to them, he conveyed through a third party to Abercromby, the English Ambassador, a sad letter, in which, retracting his generous declarations, he said he was ready to accept the frontier of the Adige, with Parma and Modena, if Austria would make the proposal to him directly, or through the medium of England (7th July).

Manin's mistrust seemed, therefore, but too well justified. Charles Albert, however, excused himself in his own eyes by the thought that Venice, abandoned by Piedmont, would take refuge under the protection of France. It never formed any part of his intentions to deliver her up to Austria.*

Mr. Abercromby, who was very favourable to the Italian cause, and who, on the 2nd of July, had even written to Lord Palmerston, expressing his opinion that it was indispensable that Austria should entirely surrender Italy—had, to his great regret, induced this step on the part of the King of Sardinia. When he saw matters in Italy growing worse and worse, and anticipating the result of the 23rd of June in France, he had urged Charles Albert seriously to examine his position, and consider what it was possible or right for him to do. Without expressing any opinion as to the personal views of the King, he limited himself to replying, that he would communicate them to his government.

The letter of Charles Albert, it must be admitted, was attended with no results. His ministers protested, his heart protested with them against himself, and the negociation was not entered upon. Besides, Austria would have

* Manin himself interpreted the conduct of the King in this manner.

refused. Its hopes were higher now. Charles
Albert was enfeebled, Austria was strengthened.
The days of June had struck the French Republic at the heart; and Hungary, by a false
calculation, which cost it very dear, Hungary—
in actual quarrel, but not yet in open rupture
with Austria—still sustained Austria in Italy.*
Radetsky assumed the offensive for the second

* This was the greatest error in the career of Kossuth,
which many subsequent brilliant actions have not repaired. The Hungarian Chamber of Representatives
wished to refuse its aid to Austria, and to recall from
Italy the troops belonging to the kingdom of Hungary;
Kossuth, then minister, was opposed to this, and made
it a cabinet question. "They tell us to recall our troops
from Italy; but do not forget, that along with
12,000 Hungarians that are there, we shall bring back
35,000 Croats!"—*Vienna Gazette*, Aug. 2nd. Kossuth's idea was, that by keeping the Slavic troops of
Hungary employed in Italy, the Magyar revolution would
be accomplished with less difficulty. Hungary learned,
when too late, that a revolution which asserted the principle of nationality would never be supported by a vio-
lation of national right, and that it was only by the
union of the peoples that they could be freed. We must
observe that Kossuth was even accused of losing Hungary
by breaking with the Austrian monarchy: the true accusation against him is just the reverse—he deferred
his breach with it too long.

time, under much more favourable conditions
than at the end of May. After five days' fighting
(22nd to 26th July), during which the Piedmontese soldiers and their leaders bravely sustained the honour of the Italian arms to the last,
the superior strategy of the enemy, who was
skilfully massed, decided the victory : the long,
weak line of the Piedmontese was broken, and
all their positions lost. Charles Albert was
compelled to order a retreat.

On the 27th of July, General Welden, who
commanded the Austrian corps of observation
before Venice, wrote to the new Provisional Government of Venice, exaggerating the sad truth
a little, that the army of Charles Albert was
completely destroyed, and that "now was the
moment, and the last, to make terms for their
cause before it was entirely lost." To this proposal to capitulate, the Venetian Government,
presided over by Castelli, replied in terms worthy
of Manin, " that even though the cause should
be reduced to the single city of Venice," he hoped
" to prove that it was yet far from being lost !"

Ten days passed, full of doubtful news, alarm,
and trouble. The people were in a state of

fermentation ;* the army was uneasy.   The republican party commenced to meet and plan.
Manin proposed the meeting of a popular assembly
to ask the Provisional Government' to organize
a committee of defence.   The government deferred its reply, and announced that it referred
the question to the Provincial Assembly of
Venice, but it secretly put itself in communication with Manin for another object, of the
highest importance.   Manin was charged to go
and consult with the French Consul respecting
the serious measures the government projected
with regard to the French Republic (2nd August).
" France! France!" was the universal cry.

On the 4th of August, the President of the
Government, Castelli, and Paolucci one of his
colleagues, announced to the French Consul the
sending of an address soliciting the aid of

* The physical sufferings of the people also added
to the moral suffering.   For some time previously provisions had become scarce and dear, and money was
deficient.   M. Vasseur writes in his *Journal,* that but
for the Artesian wells sunk by M. Degoussé, a French
engineer, the city must have capitulated for want of
water, as it was impossible to obtain any from the
mainland.

France, without waiting for the authorization of
Charles Albert. If the union with Piedmont
could not be maintained, they had prepared a
second act, by which Venice gave itself to
France, and if France refused, then to England,
rather than again bend beneath the Austrian
yoke.

On the 27th July, while Charles Albert was
retiring before the victorious enemy, the Piedmontese chambers voted the acceptance of Venice
by the Crown: the Union was promulgated at
Turin on the 29th, under the form of a law
of the United States.   On the 7th of August,
the Provisional Government of Venice resigned
its functions, and the Commissioners of the
King of Sardinia took possession of the city in
the name of Charles Albert.

Under what circumstances, alas! and in presence of what gloomy attitude of the people
and army, the official celebration of North-
Italian fusion took place!   The Neapolitan
soldiers, who had observed the bad feeling con-
sequent upon the fusion, requested to be sent
back to their own country.   Most of them embarked on the 9th of August, a few only re-

mained among the volunteers.   The latter, on the contrary, rose up exasperated.   Sinister rumours ran through the city, the gloomiest of which did not exceed the reality.

The battle lost, Charles Albert at first thought of putting the Po between himself and the enemy, which would have been good strategy—and his heaviest artillery had defiled past Plaisance, when, being informed that the Milanese had despatched to Paris the Marquis Guerrieri, member of the republican minority of the ex-Provisional Government, to claim the aid of France, he decided to go and cover Milan, disavow the mission of Guerrieri, and despatch the Marquis Ricci to Paris, charged with proposing the eventuality of intervention, but without formally demanding it.   It was only on the 3rd of August that he resigned himself to soliciting the immediate entry of a French army, on condition that " France would not claim Savoy as a compensation :" that is to say, that France should shed her blood and spend her gold to aid Italy to constitute herself by virtue of the principle of nationality, and at the same time leave a fragment of French nationality in the hands of an Italian prince by virtue of the principle of feudal inheritance.

The communication was made on the 7th of August. Before France received it, the catastrophe was accomplished.

On the 4th of August Charles Albert was before Milan, followed by Radetzky. The spirit and aspect of Milan were absolutely the same as in the great struggle of March. A committee of defence, organised on the 28th of July, had substituted its energy for the weakness of the Provisional ex-Government. The men of March re-appeared, and, among them, an heroic chief of the partisans, recently arrived from America, who seemed to be the genius of revolutionary war—GARIBALDI.

Milan was ready for a defence like that of Saragossa—of a Saragossa sustained by an army. Unfortunately, the army was not animated by the same spirit as the city. The Piedmontese army numbered only twenty-five thousand exhausted and discouraged men; and they were followed by thirty-five thousand victorious foes, who in two hours might be increased to sixty thousand. Attacked by the

Austrians in sight of Milan, the Piedmontese defended themselves courageously, but without enthusiasm; they retired upon the city. The King entered it in the afternoon, hesitating, troubled, and tortured with grief. He held a council of war. He was informed that the Milanese would not fight, that the munitions of his army were exhausted, and that in Milan there were neither money, provisions, nor stores. Now, there were more than two millions in the treasury, without reckoning the church and private plate taken in large quantities to the Mint. There were large quantities of provisions which had been collected by the Committee of Defence, and munitions of war sufficient to last many months !*

During the night the unfortunate king sent a flag of truce to Radetzky. The latter would only promise to respect the persons and property of the Milanese. At the news of this deplorable treaty, the Council of Defence uttered cries of

* The Austrian generals told the English Vice-Consul, Mr. Campbell, that they found so many stores that they did not know what to do with them: they were obliged to throw them into the canals.

indignation.   On the morning of the 5th, the
people, furious and wild, rose *en masse*, and
surrounded the palace where the King lodged.
Charles Albert promised to break the capitulation. But, during this time, anarchy had broken
out in the city and the army. The troops began
to quit the city, either of their own accord, or
at the instigation of the authors of the treaty.
The *émeute* continued amid cries of " treason !"
The vigorous Committee of Defence, and the
municipality, composed of men unequal to the
circumstances, whom it was wrong to leave in
power, acted at cross-purposes.   Amid this
chaos, the King lost his presence of mind, and
set out during the night with his army.

Everything was deranged and overthrown :
the Committee of Defence could not even attempt
to re-organize the struggle. The municipality
announced that Radetzky had granted them
until eight in the morning for those to quit the
city who wished (6th of August).   Then was
witnessed a spectacle unparalleled in the history
of the modern world.   One half the population,
women, children, and old men, abandoned their
homes, bearing their sick with them, so that

they might not die among their enemies. Many among the Milanese lost their senses!

On the afternoon of the 10th of August, a detachment of Welden's corps opened fire against the fort of Malghera; the Venetian garrison dismounted four of the enemy's cannon, and silenced the Austrian batteries.

On the morning of the 11th of August, General Welden* communicated to the Piedmontese commissioners at Venice an armistice, signed on the 9th, at Milan, by which Charles Albert engaged to evacuate all the places situated beyond his own former states, COMPRISING THE CITY OF VENICE AND THE VENETIAN TERRA FIRMA. Persons and property in the places so specified were "put under the protection of the Imperial government."

* He came from Bologna, where he had made a dash, on the 7th and 8th of August. Bologna, summoned to surrender, resisted. Welden commanded it from the heights of Montagnola. The people made a sortie, and, seconded by the peasants, took the heights by assault, and compelled the Austrian corps to retreat. This successful offensive movement of an unwarlike population attacking regular troops is a fine and rare incident in military history.

The Piedmontese reactionary party were triumphant. They had induced Charles Albert to sacrifice Italy in order to avoid French intervention, and to keep Savoy.

Manin saw · his worst anticipations realized. Having foreseen everything, he was ready to brave everything.

On the 8th of August, he received certain information of the fall of Milan. On the morning of the 9th, Manin received from Castellani, the Venetian *Chargé-d'Affaires* at Rome, a letter, dated the 5th, in which the envoy warned him of the rumour of an armistice which would surrender Venice.* "Keep on the alert," said this brave Venetian to Manin. "If the news is confirmed, proclaim it treason, constitute yourselves a republic, and call in the aid of France."

Manin hastened immediately to Cibrario, the Piedmontese author, one of the three commissioners of Charles Albert.

"If King Charles Albert were obliged, with

---

* Thus the Salasco armistice was foreseen at Rome four days before being signed.

the dagger at his throat, to give up Venice to Austria," said Manin, "what would you do?"

"The supposition is absurd and impossible!"

"Absurd and impossible it may be! I trust it is so. But we live in times when it is not useless to anticipate the absurd and impossible. Will you, then, reply to my question?"

"Venice has united herself to Piedmont to be governed and defended. If the King has not the means of governing and defending her, then the motive by which Venice gave herself to Piedmont disappears, and she returns to a state of independence, as before the fusion."

"So, then, you would not give us up to the Austrians?"

"I would rather cut myself to pieces!"

"You would, perhaps, even disobey the express order of the King?"

"It will not be disobedience. I have accepted from my government the commission to take possession of Venice and govern it. If a new commission is sent to me, I am free to accept or refuse it, and I tell you I shall refuse it."

"And what are the views of Colli* on this subject?"

"I have not questioned him as to this contingency, which appears to me impossible; but I know enough to affirm that he will be of the same opinion as myself."

Manin embraced him and departed.† He was convinced by the manner of the honest Piedmontese. Certain that he had no treason to apprehend, he waited. ‡

Meanwhile M. Paolucci took to the French consul the demand for succour announced on the 4th, and written in the name of the Provi-

* The Piedmontese General Colli, colleague of Cibrario. His four sons were in the army. One of them died for Italy in this campaign. The third commissioner was the Venetian Castelli, ex-president of the fusionist provisional government.

† Report to the Piedmontese ministry by the Commissioner Cibrario.

‡ Manin had previously (in July) put a similar question to General Pepe, "If King Charles Albert orders you to abandon Venice, what will you do?" "I shall do as I did when the Bourbon ordered me to abandon the Italian cause—disobey."

sional Government, which was in authority until the 7th.

Early in the morning of the 11th, the royal commissioners, as before stated, received notice of the armistice from General Welden. They refused either to receive a communication trans-mitted by an enemy and not by their govern-ment, or to suspend hostilities. Although fore-seeing a terrible popular explosion, when the fatal news should become known, they allowed the small corps of Piedmontese troops, recently arrived, to remain in their barracks, wishing to avoid in any case the spilling of Venetian blood, preferring to expose themselves defenceless to the first shock of the people's wrath. They immediately convoked the Venetian Council, composed of five members, with whom they shared the power, and declared to it that, if the news should unfortunately prove true, they would never consent to be the instruments of the surrender of Venice.

"We consider," they said, "our commission ended from the hour in which we shall be offi-cially informed of such a stipulation. From that moment Venice will be free to act as she may

consider most expedient both for her own cause
and for that of Italy. At that time we shall
offer her our services as simple citizens, while
regretting that we cannot do more."

"Such a stipulation," added the Commissioner Castelli, with energy, "will be nullified
by the very act of fusion, which interdicts the
disposal of the destiny of the country without
the consent of the Council. If the conditions
of the fusion are not complied with, the fusion
is null and void, and the sovereignty of the
Republic will be considered as having never
ceased."

The two Piedmontese commissioners, ad-
hering to the declaration of the Venetian, proposed some measures of military precaution;
and it was decided to convoke the Assembly of
the province of Venice on the morrow of the
day upon which they received official notice of
the armistice.

The legal question was disposed of; every
one had displayed good feeling; but, in fact,
what with these delays and legal scruples, this
waiting for an official notice which might be
delayed some days, they were very far from the

exigencies of one of those crises in which minutes reckon for days!

The meeting felt this, and recognizing their true position, dispatched Castelli to Manin.

The ex-leader of the fusion met the republican chief by announcing that he came to consult with him as to taking prompt and decisive measures.   Any one holding such language quickly came to an understanding with Manin. The day was advancing; they appointed a meeting at the government palace for eight in the evening.

Manin secretly concerted with M. Vasseur, the French consul, a man both candid and shrewd, and of a firm character, who never separated the cause of France from that of Italy, and who, to the last day, gave proofs of the most active and vivid sympathy for Venice.

The army and the city murmured like a rising tempest. The armistice had transpired. The people, whose instincts were always in harmony with the mind of its chosen leader, hurried in crowds to the residence of the French consul. M. Vasseur replied to the deputations of the people and civic guard, as he had replied to

Manin and to other notable persons, that he
had no doubts of the good feeling of his government.

Between six and seven in the evening the
Square of St. Mark was filled by an excited
crowd. Manin watched the popular movement
with great anxiety, fearing that the explosion
would effect what he was most anxious to
avoid.

"News! news!" cried the multitude with
increasing irritation. It endeavoured to force
its way into the government palace, and was
only prevented by the civic guard with great
difficulty. A secretary of the commissioner
Colli made his appearance on the balcony of the
palace. His evasive words excited louder cla-
mour. Colli and Cibrario next came out. Colli
declared that he had not received any official
news, but admitted that there was reason to
fear that the rumoured misfortunes were true.

"What! the armistice true?—And the conditions?—And the fleet?—And ourselves?"

Colli hesitated. Then these words escaped
from his lips:—

"Whatever happens, the Sardinian fleet will

remain Sardinian, the Venetian fleet will remain Venetian."

This was admitting that the King of Sardinia abandoned Venice. A fearful uproar ensued.

" We are betrayed !"—" Death to the commissioners !"—" Down with the royal government !"—" We'll have Manin !"—" Long live Manin, the Saviour of our country !"

The palace was invaded. The boldest of the men of the people and Lombard, Roman, and Venetian volunteers penetrated even to the hall in which the two Piedmontese commissioners were sitting. They were surrounded and threatened.

Brave in the presence of an *émeute* as on the field of battle, the aged Colli roused himself into a state of irritation. At this moment Manin appeared. He addressed Colli, extending his hand to him.

" Who are you ?" said Colli.

" I am Manin."

" What do you wish me to do ?"

Manin had no time to reply. The crowd replied for him.

" We wish you to resign ! We want no king!"

"I would rather be torn to pieces," replied Colli, "than resign before official news is received."

The volunteers seized Colli and Cibrario, and led them towards the window, to compel them to make their resignation from the balcony in presence of the assembled multitude. Manin rescued Colli from their hands. Castelli, the third commissioner, arrived and showed himself from the balcony.

"Resign! resign!"

"I am a Venetian! I am no longer the King's commissioner!"

"The others, then!—the others!"

Castelli turned to Manin, and begged him to address a few words to the people from the balcony.

"Yes—speak to them!" said Colli.

Castelli drew Manin to the window.

"The commissioners have not betrayed us!" cried Manin to the multitude. "I will stake my head upon their patriotism. Calm yourselves and grant me a few minutes to consult with them."

A thunder of applause was the response.

Manin held council with the three commissioners and with the French consul, who had
hastened to an interview which he had expected.
The two Piedmontese persisted in refusing to
make their official resignation, but declared that
they would henceforth abstain from acting,
and that Manin might do as he thought best.
Manin offered to share a new government with
them.   They considered this honour incompatible with their mission, not yet legally terminated.

At the expiration of half an hour Manin re-
appeared on the balcony.

" I come to assure you that France listens
more willingly to the appeal of the people, than
to the appeal of a king.   The royal commissioners declare, that from this moment they
will abstain from governing ; the assembly of
the city and province of Venetia will meet the
day after to-morrow, and nominate the new
government.   Till then, during the next forty-
eight hours," (and his voice assumed a tone
that thrilled every heart,) " till then, I WILL
GOVERN ! (*governero io !*)"

Loud shouts of joy made the square of St.

Mark echo again. The people believed itself already saved, because Venice was to be watched over by their Manin. They shouted " Long live Manin !—To the forts !—To arms !"

Manin replied :

" The drums will beat to arms, and the civic guard will muster; a certain number of citizens will be selected from each battalion; they will go this very night to the advanced posts ; to the fort of Malghera, which can repulse any attack that may be made."

But as the people continued in a state of excitement, shouting *vivas*, Manin continued :—

" My friends, if you wish me to labour for your good and safety, you must allow me to take some repose. Return to your homes ; avoid all disturbances; I shall watch over you, with my blood, with my life, if need be. Good night, my friends."

In less than ten minutes the crowd had dispersed without a murmur. There were no parties at Venice.

Manin passed the night in preparing for every contingency ; both within the city, and without.

At two o'clock in the morning, Tommaseo

and Toffoli sat out for Paris, charged by Manin to go and claim the assistance of the French Republic.

"Henceforth," said the *Gazetta di Venise* of the following day, repeating the fatal words of Charles Albert and Mazzini—" henceforth Venice will act for herself (*farà da sé*) ; she will be aided by friends and sincere allies ; Venice will be saved, and with her the sacred cause of Italy will triumph !''

Alas ! why was not this appeal made to France, who would have fully justified the confidence reposed in her, before the sinister date of the 23rd of June ! Venice might not have been saved; but her glorious misfortunes, the heroic constancy of her prolonged resistance would have secured greater victories for the future, in the cause for which she sacrificed herself !

CHAPTER VIII.

The *Triumvirate*—Appeal to France—Tommaseo at
Paris—Attitude of the Venetian People—Anglo-
French Mediation—Unfortunate basis of this media-
tion—Blockade of Venice—Offers made by Charles
Albert to Manin—Brilliant Sortie from Mestre—
Manin, Lord Palmerston, and M. Bastide—The French
Navy at Venice—Correspondence of Lord Palmerston
upon Austria—A Venetian Negociator—Valentino
Pasini—The Anglo-French Mediation.

THE policy of international isolation bore the
fruits Manin had foreseen. The counter-revolution at Naples succeeded; the foreigner tri-
umphed upon the Adige. After the fall of Milan,
as after the fall of Vicenza, Venice remained
erect. Manin endeavoured to repair the disasters caused by a policy opposed to his own;
compelling it, finally, to bring about that French

intervention, which might preserve all that was still undestroyed, and raise up all that was fallen. In any case, he would make of Venice, even if she should be abandoned and left alone by the world, an example which should for ever prevent the Italian name from falling into its past humiliation. Whatever might be the immediate issue of the struggle, he would give to an Italian city the imperishable honour of personifying the principle destined to constitute the public law of a new Europe—national independence.

On the morning that followed this night so full of heroic emotions, the dictator put himself in communication with the people and the army, by two proclamations, which were admirable commentaries upon the *Governeró io* of the previous evening—

" FELLOW CITIZENS.

" In the hour of peril, we must make prompt and bold resolutions !

" In order that you should not be left without a governor, I have not hesitated to assume, for a few hours only, the heavy responsibility of government.

" Necessity has imposed on me the office : your affection will make its execution easy !"

He announced the convocation of the Assembly on the morrow, and concluded by saying—

"Rely upon Providence, on yourselves, on Italy, on the aid of other free peoples, already invoked, and who cannot fail us."

" ITALIAN SOLDIERS.

" . . . . Our lagoons are perhaps the sole refuge of Italian liberty. In the name of that Italy for which you have fought and still desire to fight, let nothing cool your ardour for the defence of the sacred asylum of our nationality ! This is a solemn hour, it involves the political existence of all our nation : the destinies of that nation may be decided upon this, its last defence.

" Soldiers ! all you who have come from beyond the Po, Ticino, and the Mincio to make the common cause triumph ; remember that in preserving Venice, you preserve the most sacred rights of our native land.   Europe will admire and recompense you, and on the day when Italy will finally be delivered, amid the hosts of monuments that attest the valour and glory of our fathers, it will raise another monument, on which will be inscribed these words,

" ' *In defending Venice, Italian soldiers saved the independence of all Italy.*' "

On the following day, the 13th of August, Venice arose in high glee. The official gazette announced that two Venetians, arrived from Turin and Genoa, brought news of the French intervention and the immediate passage of the Alps by General Lamoricière, at the head of fifty thousand men.

It was under this impression that the provincial Venetian assembly was opened. Manin explained, simply and forcibly, the events of the previous evening, and concluded by stating the necessity for forming a purely provisional government to maintain peace within and defence from without.

"If things happen to change, then the assembly will be again convoked to decide what shall be the future of Venice, what form of government shall be chosen, or, rather, to which Italian state she shall unite herself; but during the provisional government our only political idea must be that of repulsing the enemy.   We must recognize only two parties—Italians and Austrians.   We are all Italians here!   Let us remain united now and for ever."

They proposed that he should retain the dictatorship.   He would not accept it, on the plea that he was ignorant of military affairs.   They proposed to associate with him a naval and a military colleague.   He then accepted.

" Since you show you have confidence in me," he said.   " Well, then, I shall ask, I shall demand proofs, very great proofs of this confidence.   Our cause cannot triumph except by very great sacrifices.   These sacrifices I must impose on you.   If you will not submit to them, you will do well to dismiss me at once."

" To save one's country," he added, a moment afterwards, " we must risk every thing, even the curses of our contemporaries."

By an unanimous shout of adhesion the assembly pledged itself to follow him to the last.

The triumvirate was composed of Manin, as president, of Admiral Graziani, and Colonel Cavedalio.   The two latter, notwithstanding their advanced age, were very active ; both were

honourable and devoted; and the second, the
colonel, possessed all that vigour of character
necessary to maintain order in an army composed of divers elements, very difficult to manage.

A deputy proposed that the president should
be bound to convoke the assembly whenever
requested to do so by a certain number of representatives.   Manin replied that neither himself
nor his colleagues would remain in power a moment after they perceived that the confidence of
their fellow-citizens was weakened or lost; but as
they had desired a dictatorship, he must arrange
the conditions of it, and allow the government
to judge of the fit occasions upon which to have
recourse to the assembly.

The assembly acquiesced in this; then voted
the ratification of the appeal made to France,
and sent a special envoy with a message to this
effect to the French government.   Manin declared that, if negociations were opened, Venice
ought not to argue the legal title of the capitulation signed by an Austrian commander on the
22nd of March, but solely on the right of its
indefeasible nationality—on the right of every

people to recover their invaded independence.
"Nations, at the present day, no longer value
the old arguments of diplomacy."

He terminated the sitting by making it vote,
in the name of Venice—as a duty more indispensable than ever under present circumstances
—their warmest thanks to the Piedmontese
people, whose brave army had endured so much
suffering and shed so much blood in support of
the common cause.

He had previously required a declaration of
esteem and affection in favour of the Piedmontese commissioners, as a just amends for the
trials they had endured.

Thus, from amid reverses, the usual sources
of discord, he laboured to elicit union and fraternity.

The commissioners were worthy of the sentiments expressed by Manin. Early on the
morning of the 12th of August, the commander
of a Sardinian vessel at anchor opposite the
arsenal hastened to General Colli, offering his
services and those of his men to protect him
against the popular hostility. "We are on a
good understanding with Manin," replied Colli.

" He has given us his word, and that is sufficient."

The Sardinian admiral, Albani, on his part,
wrote to say, that so long as he did not receive
a formal order from his government to withdraw, he should continue to defend Venice.

Manin charged Mengaldo, the commander of
the civic guard, with bearing the message of the
Venetian assembly to Paris. " Citizen minister,"
he wrote to M. Bastide, the minister for foreign
affairs, " our peril is extreme.   Our nationality
and independence rest henceforth upon the
prompt succour accorded to us by the free
people of France."   (14th of August.)   At the
same time he wrote to the French ambassador
at Rome, praying him to permit the admiral
commanding the Mediterranean squadron, then
in the Sicilian waters, and which had recently
interposed between the King of Naples and the
Sicilians, to send some vessels of war to Venice.

At home, the triumvirate made its *début* by
reorganizing the committees of vigilance and
defence.   A decree of the 16th of August ordered that every article of gold and silver should
be sent to the mint within the next eight-and-

forty hours, in exchange for a receipt bearing
interest at five per cent.   Non-compliance with
this decree entailed the confiscation of the objects
not presented, besides a day's imprisonment for
every hundred lire in value not declared.   This
was a rigorous measure.   Manin wished it to
remain a moral obligation, and refused to encourage informers by a recompense.

Intimidation was unnecessary.   The whole
population, without distinction of class, hastened
to the *zecca,* or mint, not with resignation, but
with heroic gaiety.

Other decrees mobilized the civic guard, and
ordered a general enrolment of the citizens from
eighteen years of age to forty.   The civic guards,
mobilized for the garrisons, went to the forts as
gaily as to a festival; and all this was done
without the least tumult or disorder, but with a
serenity and dignity truly admirable.

Nevertheless the news which on the 13th of
August had spread joy over Venice was not
confirmed.   Instead of immediate intervention,
the foreign journals brought rumours of an
Anglo-French mediation, based, as they expressed it, on Italian independence; but, al-

though the language of the French press was encouraging, Manin, who saw the representative of Lord Palmerston at Venice act as an Austrian rather than an English consul, and who had no means of divining the very different part which the English minister was acting, was disposed to view with deep distrust any combination in which the " Foreign Office " had a share.

He made a great effort with the English minister. On the 20th of August, he addressed a private letter to Lord Palmerston, which is a masterpiece of true diplomacy, and in which he endeavoured to convince by the light of truth and eloquent reasoning. Addressing the representative of a traditional government, he relied upon historic rights; demonstrated the complete illegality of everything which had been done with regard to Venice since 1797, and the positive right the Venetians possessed to re-establish the legal government which existed prior to the treaty of Campo Formio. He detailed the events that had happened since the 22nd of March; and referred to the rumours in circulation respecting the intentions of the French and English governments, which, it was said, had made proposals to Austria, and were prepared, in case of refusal, to have recourse to arms. He intreated the English minister to take measures to insist on the suspension of hostilities against the Venetians while the negociations continued, as they were against Piedmont by the armistice of the 9th of August, thus leaving the Austrians at liberty to throw all their forces on Venice. Lastly, he implored him not to allow a people to fall again under the Austrian yoke, which they detested, and to which they could never become resigned, but against which they would continually rise, to the great risk of the peace of Europe; their fixed determination was to unite themselves with the other Italian peoples, and to separate for ever from the Germans.

He concluded by observing that the economical interests of Italy were favourable to free trade, " a theory to which Austria, consulting only the interests of its manufacturers, had always shown itself hostile."

On the same day, two other despatches from Manin were sent, one to Turin, the other to Paris. In the first, Manin explained to the

Sardinian minister for foreign affairs, the character of the new Venetian government, as
purely provisional, and for the public safety,
and which left all anterior or future political
questions intact. " Venice," he said, " has not
forgotten, and never will forget, what Charles
Albert, his army, and his people, the Liguri-
Piedmontese people, have done for the cause
of Italian independence. The profoundest gratitude is engraven on the hearts of all : reverses,
so far from weakening it, have, on the contrary, augmented it : everyone yet hopes that
the champion of Italy will not restore his generous sword to its scabbard, but that he will soon
raise the fortunes of the holy war."

" So long as Venice remains free," he added,
"the cause of Italian liberty will not be lost ;"
and he begged the Sardinian government, in the
event of Anglo-French mediation, to interpose
for the armistice to be extended to Venice, and
also to send to the Venetian government a sum
of money, despatched before the armistice, and
also the muskets bought in France, which
had arrived at Genoa after many delays.

The other letter was addressed to Tommaseo,

envoy from Venice to Paris. It also insisted upon including Venice in the armistice.

"If even the political condition of Venice should be considered as a question yet to be debated in the negociations, still it must not be permitted that its present condition be changed during the course of the negociations. . . . But the independence of Venice should not be called in question; it ought to be stated as a previous condition. . . . France has an immense debt to repay to Venice: it must repair the iniquity of Campo Formio: it would cover itself with shame and curses, if in these days the same iniquity were repeated by it, or through its connivance."*

At the moment Manin sent off these despatches, he received a letter of the deepest interest from Florence. It was from M. Tom-

---

* M. Vasseur, the French consul, under this date, Aug. 20th, entered in his journal the following words which he heard spoken around him, "Even though we shall be crushed, we shall continue to fight, until certain that France abandons us. She will see that we are worthy of all her sympathy."

Venice more than kept its word. It continued to fight even after it was certain of being abandoned!

maseo Gar, one of his agents in France, who
on the evening of the 9th of August left Paris,
to inform Manin of the real intentions of the
French government. Gar informed him of the
contre-coup produced in Paris by the Piedmontese reverses. The Marquis Ricci, envoy from
Charles Albert, had commenced by baffling the
mission of Guerrieri, who demanded immediate
succour in the name of the Milanese. The
Piedmontese minister protested that the fusion
of Upper Italy being now accomplished, he was
sole representative of Lombardy, as of Piedmont,
and that his king did not ask for immediate
intervention; but on the 7th of August, upon
new instructions arriving from Turin, the Marquis Ricci at length made the request before
mentioned : a request accompanied by so strange
a reservation. The French government replied
that it was too late, and that France could only
offer a mediation in conjunction with England.
This terrible blow determined the envoys from
Milan and Venice * to make next day a despair-

* Manin's agents had been confirmed by the Fusionist government.

s 2

ing appeal to General Cavaignac, entreating him
to save Milan, which, alas, had fallen two days
previously, and to protest against the diplomatic concert of France with the English
government, which, as they believed, was negociating with Austria without France, and against
her.

Cavaignac replied that, in consequence of internal disorders, and of the derangement of its
finances, France must avoid provoking a European war by an armed intervention in Italy ; that
he had first satisfied himself of the intentions of
England ;* and having found her disposed to
interfere between Italy and its enemies, he had,
that very day, sent two commissioners to Turin
and Vienna, to propose an armistice, and a
satisfactory arrangement : that if the armistice
or the mediation were rejected by Austria,
France would then immediately interfere by its
arms.

" Upon our enquiring what was the basis of
the mediation proposed by France, he replied :—

* In the " *Correspondence*" we perceive that the
French government had, on the 22nd of July, made
formal overtures to England for a mediation in common.

" 'The independence of Upper Italy :—a pecuniary indemnity satisfactory to Austria.'

" The conversation afterwards turned upon
the probability of the fall of Milan, and of the
atrocious revenge the vanquishers would prac-
tise ; Cavaignac added resolutely :—

" ' Make your minds easy.   Milan will never
remain Austrian.'

" ' And Venice,—will you allow Venice to be
sacrificed anew ?'

" ' Certainly not.   Everything that depends
on us shall be done, to prevent such a misfortune !'

" Upon that," added Gar, " he took leave of
us, and I resolved to set out immediately, in
order to acquaint you with his language, and
with these facts : and I beg of you to prepare
for protesting energetically by arms, in the event
of France giving way to the pretensions of Austria, and to the counsel of England,* ever con-
senting to sign a new treaty of Campo Formio."

---

* These prejudices against the English government
were almost universal.   We have seen what were its
real dispositions.

While the Venetian envoy started on his journey under the shock of these painful apprehensions, on the 9th of August, M. Bastide, the French minister for foreign affairs, and Lord Normanby, the English Ambassador at Paris, mutually arranged the basis of the mediation to be proposed to the Emperor of Austria and the King of Sardinia. These were :—

The immediate suspension of hostilities between the Austrian and Italian troops.

The formal renunciation, on the part of Austria, of all right of sovereignty over Lombardy : the present constitution of the government of Northern Italy, the result of the wishes expressed by the Lombards being a fact to be taken as the basis of the mediation, without the ulterior guarantee of the two mediating powers.

AUSTRIA TO RETAIN THE SOVEREIGNTY OF VENETIA, with a similar constitution to that of Hungary, and a separate government and administration.

A special convention for Parma and Modena.

This was nothing more nor less than the Hummelauër proposal.

The English diplomatic correspondence in-

forms us, that on the 22nd of July the French
government had requested the British Cabinet
to take this proposal as the starting point of a
united mediation ; Lord Palmerston then stated
the reply he had given to M. Hummelauër — a
reply which insisted on the protection of Venice.
It was then agreed that this reply should be taken
as the basis of the mediation, but when subsequent events greatly altered the position for the
worse, it was determined to revert to the Austrian proposal, but with a manifest reluctance on
the part of Lord Palmerston.*

The " *Independence* " promised by General
Cavaignac was therefore only an Italian administration under a foreign monarchy ! The new
French government, in its relations with Venice,
always energetically protested against the being
suspected of any desire to re-enact another
Campo Formio; they had no intention, in fact,

* Correspondence respecting the affairs of Italy.
State Papers, 1849, part iii. p. 60—122. In comparing
the respective attitudes of the English and French governments, it is proper not to forget that England undertook only to sustain the Italian cause *morally;* while with
France, the result of a rejected mediation was to be war.

of delivering up Venice unconditionally to Austrian brutality ; they intended to make the police and militia of Austria quit Venetia, and allow a viceroy to enter it ; at the bottom of their refusal to guarantee the union of Lombardy and Piedmont was the wish to effect the union of Lombardo-Venetia in a single state under the suzerainty of Austria. They did not suppose that Venetia would remain for ever subjected to the Austrian empire ; but they considered it would be more likely to escape by remaining united to Lombardy, and that a regime of transition would pave the way for real independence on the first favourable opportunity.

Previous to the last revolutions of France and Italy, this system, under the form of a concession accorded by Austria, would have been for the time acceptable ; but just because it would have proved acceptable, Austria, very clearly foreseeing the consequences, would never have granted it. It had ceased to be acceptable, from the moment that rivers of blood, and still more even than that blood, the solemn demand of the absolute right of nationality, separated Italy from Austria. Italy, armed and stipulating for itself, would not, could not, accept what subjugated Italy had submitted to.   Besides, it might be assumed that Austria, reanimated by the successes of Radetzky, would not now consent to these bases, and that any negociation with it would be a snare. The French Revolution brought an incalculable amount of odium by disposing of a people without consulting them, and by engaging in negociations contrary to its principles, which could result only in deplorable deceptions or a lingering war.

Manin did not know of this grave error of the French government; but with grief he had foreseen it.   On receipt of the letter from Gar, he judged it indispensably necessary that Venice should be represented at the approaching negociations; for this delicate mission he selected M. Valentino Pasini, a humble advocate of Vicenza, in whom he had recognized superior qualities.   He instructed him to reject absolutely, in the name of Venice and the Venetian provinces: 1st. Every kind of dependence, direct or indirect, on the Austrian Empire.   2nd. A monarchy, even an independent one, under a prince of the house of Austria, or one of the branch of Este (Modena). " Any other combination will be accepted by us," he wrote; " the kingdom of Upper Italy, the Lombardo-Venetian State, or Venice as a separate State." (23rd of August.)

Manin, in concert with his two colleagues, took the most energetic measures for defence. A decree of the 31st of August opened a national loan of ten millions of lire (£340,000), "intended to sustain the insurrection in the Lombardo-Venetian provinces; to defend Venice, and in maintaining the independence of that city, to preserve the liberty and honour of all Italy."

The debt was declared to be guaranteed by all the Lombardo-Venetian provinces, by virtue of an engagement entered into by the Lombard provisional ex-government, to guarantee, concurrently with Venice, all the debts that might be contracted for the war of independence. The defence committee of Lombardy, which had taken refuge on Swiss territory, had sent Cæsar Correnti as delegate to Venice, who ratified this declaration.*

On the 5th of September, the little corps of

* This is the same M. Correnti who in 1859 wrote the address from the Piedmontese Chamber of Deputies to the King.

Piedmontese troops remaining at Venice reim-
barked.   The Sardinian squadron set sail on the
9th.   Admiral Albini had delayed his departure
as long as he possibly could ; his own sentiments
were in harmony with the earnest entreaties of
the Venetians, and with those of the French
consul, and of the commander of the French
naval station, M. Ricaudy ; but he was at last
obliged to execute the conditions of the unfortunate armistice.   The Venetian triumvirate
had enjoyed nearly a month's respite, which it had
employed in putting the place into a formidable
state of defence.   Beside the military organization of the population,* volunteers had been
invited from all parts to reinforce the troops of
the line, and the land forces found themselves
numerically stronger than before the departure
of the Piedmontese.   There were about 20,000
soldiers.

Meanwhile M. Pasini sat out on his special
mission. Tommaseo, the eminent man who represented the Venetian republic at Paris, wrote
to Manin, that the unexpected resistance of

* Venice and the towns of the lagoons numbered
about 180,000 souls.

Venice had produced a strong impression, and
that in political circles there was some talk of
recognizing the independence of Venice like a
Hanseatic town, at the same time giving an Austrian viceroy to the rest of Venetia; an arrangement which, for his own part, he energetically rejected.   He announced that the French Government had sent to Vienna, on the 24th of August,
an appeal to the Austrian government to accept
the Anglo-French mediation (25th of August).

During this interval Tommaseo threw out,
beside the diplomatic appeal to the French government, a public appeal to France, in which
the noblest views were expressed in the most
eloquent language.

Other letters of Tommaseo and Mengaldo, of
the 31st of August and the 1st of September,
contained favourable anticipations.   On the 29th
of August, General Cavaignac, after questioning
Mengaldo as to the resolution of the Venetians,
and their means of resistance, told him that at
that very hour the French fleet would be before Venice;   that if Austria refused mediation
on the basis of the independence of Italy, France
would occupy Venice and declare war.

The fear that Venice would succumb before a sudden attack of the Austrians suggested to the French government the idea of occupation. A moment, and the question was decided.* Orders were sent to Toulon to embark a brigade of infantry and convey it to Venice.

It was now the 1st of September. Here is what Lord Palmerston had written previously to his ambassador at Vienna, Lord Ponsonby, upon transmitting to him a copy of the letter in which the French ambassador at London, M. Gustave de Beaumont, claimed the co-operation of Great Britain, in order to compel Austria to suspend hostilities against Venice :—

"Her Majesty's Government entirely share

* We are not certain whether it was at this moment that a politician, who certainly was not without faults, but to whom justice has not always been done—Armand Marrast, president of the Constituent—passed the whole night in showing General Cavaignac the necessity for making war to establish the Republic. On the 22d of September, Ducoux, the *préfet de police*, came to the same conclusion in a report on the state of public opinion, and of the imminent danger there was of the people and army becoming disaffected, if the policy of the previous government were resumed.

the anxious desire expressed by the French Government that the armistice which has been established between the Austrians and the Italians in other parts of Northern Italy should be considered as extending to Venice. . . . . The armistice which the British and French Government proposed was meant to include the whole of Northern Italy, and to embrace Venice as well as all other places in those parts. . . . Your Excellency will, of course, confine your official communication to a statement to this effect; but in any confidential conversation which you may have on these matters with Baron Wessenberg, you will not fail to urge him seriously to consider the very difficult position in which the French Government is placed in regard to these Italian affairs. . . . That Government is seriously desirous of maintaining peace, and disinclined to interfere in the affairs of Italy by force of arms. But it would be a most fatal mistake for the Austrian Government to suppose that France is unable so to interfere, if she was resolved to do so. . . . .

"Troops France has in abundance for such a purpose, after providing an ample force for the maintenance of order and tranquillity in her interior. Money France will always find the means of raising for the purpose of beginning a war to rescue Italy from the domination of Austria; and although public opinion now supports the Government in its avowed determination to employ negociation in preference to an appeal to arms, yet, if the French Government were to change its tone, and were to declare that negociation had failed, and that military interference had become necessary for the rescue of Italy and for the honour of France, there cannot be the slightest doubt that such an appeal to the popular passions would be answered by acclamation, and that the Government, which is now supported by the sober reason of the French nation in its present course, would be backed enthusiastically by popular applause in such an altered determination."

France, therefore, put herself in motion; and England, approving, morally sustained her. The English ambassador at Paris asked only that they should wait two or three days more for the reply of Austria to the summons addressed to it by France. (4th of September.)

The Austrian minister for foreign affairs replied to the *chargé d'affaires* of France, at
Vienna, on the 3d of September :—*

"The Imperial Government accepts the offer
of mediation made to it by the Government of
the French Republic and by that of Great Britain, *reserving to itself the arranging with the
mediating powers the conditions which must
serve as the basis of the negociation.*

"I must, however, observe beforehand, that
the negociation about to take place cannot be
based on the state of things which existed when
the Imperial Government took the initiative, in
order to put an end to hostilities. . . . .

"Austria is conscious of having done every
thing that could reasonably be required of her,
in order to maintain the peace of Europe, . . . by
limiting her successes . . . strictly to the state of
possession of the interested parties such as it is
defined by the treaties."†

* He had received the summons only on the 1st of
September.

† In several other documents it audaciously asserted
that the government of the French Republic, upon its
début, had recognized those treaties.

Thus Austria accepted the mediation, with the essential alteration of rejecting its basis, and the declaration that she would abide by the treaties of 1815.

Such an acceptance was a refusal. Unfortunately it was not so interpreted at Paris; and the order to embark the troops for Venice was countermanded.

If this illusory acceptance had not arrived in time to prevent the sailing of the expedition, the whole course of events would have been changed. The French troops once at Venice, nothing could have withdrawn them. When the 10th of December came, the new Government would have found France pledged; and the same point of military honour which, at a later period, produced such disastrous consequences, as the result of General Oudinot's " *réconnaissance* " before Rome, would in an opposite direction have caused the happiest results to Venice. The French flag would certainly not have retired.

On the 7th of September, the Venetian Government received from the French consul at Venice official notice, arrived by way of Vienna, that the mediation was accepted.

Manin immediately sent fresh instructions to the agent whom he intended to be the representative of Venice in the coming conferences. He insisted, above every thing, upon the necessity of giving to the intervention of Pasini, whether direct or indirect, in these negociations the character which belongs to the representative of an independent and free government— of a government legitimately elected by the people, and restored to full possession of the sovereign power by the annulling of the act of fusion with Piedmont. He was determined, in fact, above all things, to prevent any treaty being concluded without Venice, or in spite of her.

He reviewed the combinations which were inadmissible, and those that might be accepted. Among the latter, he placed a constitutional monarchy under the Duke of Leuchtenberg, (of whom it was said that he might reconcile France and Russia,) on condition that there should be no Russian protectorate, direct or disguised. Among the former, he excluded the isolated independence of Venice, as a Hanseatic city. The revenues of Venice were insufficient to support a navy in a state to defend her and protect her commerce; she would be obliged to seek refuge

under foreign protection, "above all other considerations, this arrangement put farther off that
confederation of the Italian states, which alone
could make of Italy an independent nation." "The
principal aim to be always kept in view," he
wrote, "must be the realization of a confederation which will make of Italy a power one and
indivisible, establish an ideal political individuality,
and blend all the divers families or Italian states
in a single moral personality, enabling it to take
its place among the nations of the world."

Among the combinations that might be accepted, the best, it appeared to him, was the
Venetian democratic republic, the re-establishment of which should be submitted to the free
vote of the provinces ; the worst would be the
kingdom of Upper Italy, because it would render
the Italian confederation very difficult, by destroying in the very outset the balance of power
(8th of September).*

---

* We must remark in this place, that Manin knew
that the French government was not at all favourable to
a kingdom of Upper Italy, and very much inclined to a
confederation of the Italian states ; this consideration
may have influenced his opinions.

On the same day, Manin wrote to Tommaseo, directing him to protest to the French government against the conduct of the Austrians, who, at the very time they accepted the mediation, took advantage of the departure of the Sardinian squadron to commence hostilities at sea, and capture the boats and vessels of Venice that were in the Gulf. He charged him to ask France either to grant, or guarantee, a loan, accepting as security a mortgage of the treasures of art at Venice.

On the 10th of September, at the conclusion of a review of the national guard, the people assembled under the windows of the government palace. Their hearts thirsted for a word from their leader; Manin simply and majestically thanked the people, the civic guard, and the Italian Volunteers for their courageous efforts and sacrifices. " If the two mediating powers," he said, " should offer (which cannot for a moment be supposed) conditions unworthy of a great and free people, Venice will do what it did on the 11th of August; it will never accept them !"

" Never ! never !" replied the whole square of St. Mark, as an immense echo.

"This, perhaps," wrote Manin to Tommaseo, "is the first true joy that I have experienced since the 22nd of March."

All classes rivalled each other in zeal ; the old aristocracy, though no longer at the head of the city, either by traditional authority or by political skill, maintained an honourable position by its patriotic sentiments ; the wealthy citizens exhibited an unbounded devotion. The government having made an appeal on account of the embarrassment in their finances, and having authorised a loan of five millions lire (£180,000), forty of the richest citizens immediately raised a loan of three millions of lire* (£100,000), part in cash, and part in commercial bills, which were discounted by the National Bank (instituted on the 25th of July, by the fusionist government) ; the bank, in order to reimburse itself, being authorised to make a special issue of notes. (19th of September.) Under foreign dominion, the people would never take the Austrian paper-money at any price :

* The expenses were upwards of 100,000 lire per day: the ordinary receipts were not more than 200,000 lire per month ; and succour from without, upon which they had a right to reckon, was not forthcoming.

the *patriotic money*, as they called the new bank-notes, they received with delight, and kissed them devoutly as sacred things.

This harmony and firmness were very necessary. The first news from Paris, since the acceptance of the mediation, was not very encouraging. Under the date of the 8th of September, Tommaseo wrote, that the conditions were not yet known, but that the French ministers spoke again of a Lombardo-Venetian kingdom, and of Venice as a Hanseatic city; and moreover, that Lombardy and Venetia would not be directly represented in the negociations Manin replied, that he must refuse everything that would be opposed to the general aim of the Italian insurrection—that is to say, to the complete independence of the country, and again rejected the idea of Venice reduced to the limits of its lagoons (19th September).

The Austrians continued their maritime aggressions; the resumption of the blockade already begun in fact, was officially announced on the 18th of September.

The French navy in the waters of Venice was at length reinforced. The French Admiral had sent, not his whole fleet, as it was hoped he

would, but a ship of the line and a frigate,
which were soon after joined by another ship of
the line; Venice did not at first derive much
advantage from their presence.   The French
navy being prohibited from attacking the Austrians, the scandalous spectacle was witnessed, of
Venetian barges seized under the very guns of
the French.   (22nd and 23rd of September.)

The Austrians projected going much further,
and seemed to be preparing for a great effort, ·
both by land and by sea.   The blood of the
French [sailors boiled with indignation.   The
French commander of the station kept secret
that he was without instructions in the event of
an attack on the part of the Austrians ; the consul aided him in this, and contrived that a rumour should reach the Austrian spies in Venice
that the French would defend the city ; at the
same time the French ships were cleared as for
action, and the commander of the station in
person, M. Ricaudy, with two steam-ships, the
Asmodee and the *Brasier*,* blockaded the point

* The name of the Captain of the *Brasier*, M. Passa-
ma, deserves to be associated with that of M. Ricaudy ;
this brave officer shared the sentiments and joined
heartily in all the acts of his chief.

of the Lido, the most favourable for a disembarcation.

The Austrian fleet appeared, but disappeared almost immediately.   The funds went down at Vienna.   Meanwhile, a nocturnal surprise against the fort of O, near Malghera, was repulsed by the Venetians (23rd—26th September).

Every project of attack on the part of the enemy was postponed; but the blockade was continued.   The French commander did not venture to exceed his instructions by giving chase to the Austrian steamers, which intercepted the communication of the Venetians with the outside.

The Austrian government cannot be accused of bad faith in this particular; three days after its strange acceptance of the mediation,* it replied in the following terms to a note from M. de La Cour upon extending the armistice to Venice :—

" . . . . The French government will ap-

* Lord Palmerston expressed himself in very strong terms on this matter in his letter of the 22d of September to Lord Ponsonby, declaring that the reply of the Austrian government was neither sufficient nor satisfactory.

preciate the difference which presents itself between a belligerent power, like his Sardinian
Majesty, and an insurgent city; an armistice
may be concluded with the one, but the other
must be quelled.

" The Imperial government declares itself
ready to grant a complete amnesty to the population of Venice, as soon as it returns under the
dominion of its legitimate sovereign."

Thus the mediation was accepted under derisory conditions: the armistice was not granted
at all.

This singular state of things was prolonged
for nearly three weeks; Austria declared as
prizes every ship conveying to Venice munitions
of war, clothing, shoes, and even provisions;
and Venice was alarmed at seeing most of the
French vessels depart.*

Manin, before making reprisals, wrote to Tommaseo to closely question the French minister,
" in order to learn if Venice might reckon upon
an effective assistance, or consider herself as

* It was the bad weather that compelled the larger
ships to leave their anchorage; M. Ricaudy always remained with the *Asmodée*.

abandoned by every one." If France replied favourably, Tommaseo was to ask her to put an end to a maritime blockade which was incompatible with the mediation, and to obtain for Venice the possibility of paying its troops, either by advance-money or by granting the guarantee of the French government on a loan. He showed how important it was to the mediating powers to maintain Venice free, either by way of modifying the pretensions of Austria, in case of peace, or of assuring the success of a war in case of a rupture.

"Time alone," he added, "will suffice to make us succumb without help. We must insist, therefore, upon receiving a positive and prompt reply; for if others wish to deceive us, *we do not wish to deceive our country.*" (10th of October.) *

He gave a fresh proof of it on the morrow. Upon the first symptoms of discontent at the inaction of the Venetian marine, he convoked

* In this same letter, wholly devoted to every Italian interest, Manin recommended to Tommaseo to combine as much as possible the cause of Sicily with that of Venice, " that equally unfortunate island."

the Provincial Assembly, to invite it first to
name a committee for the purpose of examining
into their political situation, and then a new
government, if it judged the dictatorship to be
unnecessary.

A touching incident marked the opening of
the sitting. Upon a proposal to allow a salary
to the members of the government, which had
not been given since the 13th of August, Manin
mounted the tribune. " For my part," he said,
" so long as the country is distressed, I shall
accept no salary. I will live on my own resources
as long as I can. When they are gone, I shall
have recourse to my friends, but not to a country
reduced to holding out its hand! (*una patria
mendica !*)"

The Assembly responded by a strong mark
of confidence in reversing the order of the day,
and first discussing the maintenance of the dictatorship on the reports presented by the trium-
virs, without waiting for a committee. Manin
affirmed that the position of the city was better
than when the dictatorship was proclaimed on
the 13th of August; that they had provisions
sufficient to last several months, which also

continued to arrive every day, in spite of the
blockade; and that there was no fear of any
trouble with "this good people." It was only
necessary, it appeared to him, to avoid giving
way to impatient people, who wished the government to abandon the expectant policy, "the
only one which at that moment could save
Venice, and with Venice Italy."

In fact, it was not advisable to assume the
offensive before receiving the reply of France.

Manin's colleagues, Cavedalis and Graziani,
then explained the naval and military condition
of the city. The report of Cavedalis was satisfactory. They had nearly twenty thousand men,
troops of the line, on foot, of whom nearly fourteen thousand were Venetians, and more than
six thousand Lombards, Romans, Neapolitans,
&c., with four legions of national guards, and
riflemen and artillerymen perfectly drilled. The
general command was concentrated in the hands
of General Pepe, admirably seconded by a Neapolitan officer of strong character and the highest
military capacity, the chief of the staff, Girolamo
Ulloa, one of those strong, simple natures, which
combine coolness with courage and strong com-

mon sense, and admirably suited to co-operate
with Manin. Everything had been vigorously
re-organized in the midst of continual alarms
and attempts of the enemy against the forts on
the land side.*

An interesting discussion ensued upon the
attitude to be taken by Venice in the negociations. The deputy Malfatti, without denying
the new right of Italian unity, wished to claim
the ancient right of Venice, a right against
which a brutal and iniquitous act could never
acquire the force of prescription. Radetzky,
very recently, in an address to the German diet
of Frankfort, had demanded the old dominion
of Germany over Lombardy, "at all times," he
said, "the fief of the Germanic empire:" but
he took care not to mention Venetia, which never
belonged to the Empire, and through which the
Emperor had to ask permission to pass, in order
to proceed on a visit to his "fief" of Lombardy.
"Venetia," observed Malfatti, "once free, ac-

* As to the sea, the government at this very time
made fresh efforts to buy some steamers at Genoa and
elsewhere.

cording to its ancient right, it would be impossible for Austria to retain Lombardy."

The deputy Benvenuti protested, in the name of the right which was derived from God and nature, against the appeal to historic title; and demanded that Venice should defend the rights of the whole of Italy, by claiming the fulfilment of the solemn promise given by the French nation to deliver the Italian people.

Manin restored harmony, by claiming the power of putting forward both the historic right and the right of nationality according to the time and the place, and of stipulating for Venetia without losing sight of the common cause, or surrendering the right which Venice retains of uniting herself again, if she thought proper, to Lombardy and Piedmont. " So long as Venice is free, Italy encourages hope; Venice fallen, the cause of Italy is lost."

The Assembly left the government full discretion in the negociations, reserving to itself the ratification of the final treaty. (11th of October.)

Manin, in presence of the Assembly, alluded to the possibility of a new union with Piedmont. He had received secret communications of the

highest importance.   A friend, Count Freschi,
a Venetian patriot, had written to him from
Turin in the name of Charles Albert.   (25th of
September.)   A decided revolution had taken
place in the mind of this unhappy prince.   Filled
with grief and shame, deeply irritated against
the councillors who had advised a fatal armistice,
he had now but one idea, that of reinstating
himself at any cost.   The scales had fallen from
his eyes.   He could now clearly recognise his
real enemies and those of his country in the
Austro-jesuitical party.   He was resolved to
unite himself with the patriots and democracy,
of recommencing the war at their head, and
staking every thing.   He had, it is true, accepted
the Anglo-French mediation of the 15th of
August, with the proposed bases, for what concerned him ; but after energetic protestations in
favour of Venetian independence, Austria not
having accepted the bases of the mediators, he
considered his pledged word free, and he hoped
the negociations would end in nothing.   He
now entered into a secret understanding with
the leader of the Piedmontese democratic party,
M. Brofferio, to form, among the most eminent

of the men of every Italian region a ministry
"wholly revolutionary," according to the expression of Count Freschi; and he wished particularly to offer the portfolio of foreign affairs to
Manin.

M.M. Brofferio and Freschi strongly urged
Manin to accept it. "I well know," wrote
Count Freschi, "that this would be an immense
sacrifice on your part; that it would demand a
complete abnegation of one's self to brave the
commentaries of the Square of St. Mark. But
have you done any thing else for the past seven
months than sacrifice yourself entirely for your
country? The thing to be considered is, whether you can best serve your country as triumvir
at Venice or as minister at Turin—Turin transformed, be it understood, by a revolution. The
affairs of Italy can only be improved by means
of a new and radical revolution; and both by
your talents and your loyalty you are truly the
man ordained to direct it."

The reply of Manin, which unfortunately cannot be found, left a profound impression on the
memories of the two persons who were associated with the King in this important step. It

was simple and noble. According to the testimony of M. Brofferio, the following is the substance of it:—

"Without considering myself indispensable to Venice, I nevertheless think that it is my duty to be there at the present time (*il mio donere mi vual qui*). I thank the King and the worthy citizen who has thought of me. When the safety of Italy summons me to Turin, I shall go where my country calls me."

He was deeply moved by this, though not disturbed. It was not only the citizen of Venice but the Italian statesman who decided in the negative. He wished above every thing, in negociation and in war, to save the great *place d'armes* of liberty confided to his care.

This was understood even by Piedmont, as is proved by an appeal, addressed about this time to the population, by the commission of aid to Venice, at the head of which was Gioberti, with Ratazzi, Valerio, &c.

"Help! save Venice! The keys of Italian peace or war are with Venice! Venice is not like Lombardy, which a battle or a week's march can give or take from us. Venice is even the

key of Italy on the east, without which it will
never be safe against the attacks of Austria.
Venice lost, we must reconquer it by torrents of
blood and, long years of war."

NOTE TO PAGE 34.

"GALLICIAŃ POLICY."

THE allusion to the "Gallician Policy" of Austria w¨
not be understood by those who do not remember th
events which preceded the annexation of Cracow t.
Austria, in 1846.

The province, or, as it is frequently called, the kingdom of Gallicia, is constituted of that portion of the
ancient Polish territories which, in their partition, Austria has received as her share of the prey. In the commencement of the year 1846, it was the scene of a
servile war, a rising of the peasants against the pro-
prietors, which was marked by atrocities which far
surpassed any that Paris witnessed during the worst
days of the French revolution.

The charge against the Austrian government is, that
these atrocities were excited, encouraged, and rewarded
by their agents. Unhappily for the honour of all

the women and children were in general spared, the chateaus were committed to the flames. Unknown agents everywhere presented themselves, and said, 'A few leagues hence they are massacreing your brethren.' These words were implicitly believed, and followed by a general insurrection and march against some neighbouring chateaus, when the work of conflagration and massacre was complete."

"Volumes would scarcely suffice to recount the various horrors of this disastrous insurrection, where the worst passions of human nature were brought to the aid of the infernal work of destruction. THE CRY WAS EVERYWHERE HEARD, 'WE ARE ALLOWED THREE DAYS OF LIBERTY AND PILLAGE;' and soon it was so generally acted on, that the whole country resembled a town taken by assault."

" A few tragic examples will shew the terrible nature of the revolt. Rotarski, landlord of Olasna, had been distinguished for a life of beneficence, which had deservedly won for him the title of King of the Peasants. Seized by the peasants, he asked to be allowed to confess, as he was taken past a church. 'Go on, there is no God,' cried the tigers who surrounded him. The curé of the church was brought out, and put beside him on the cart, and both were beaten with clubs, until the noble expired. Hodorynski had been concealed by his wife in a strong box, but being discovered, she supplicated them in the name of heaven to convey him to a place of safety. They feigned to comply, and putting him in a cart, harnessed the wife to it instead of the

horse, saying, ' Since you will have him in a place of
safety, drag him yourself.'   She strove to do so, and
dropped down of fatigue, while her unhappy husband
was beat to death by her side with clubs.   The fate of
Brosinskwi is still more frightful.   They cut off his nose,
tongue, and ears, scooped out his eyes, and cut off all
his fingers before he died.   His wife was compelled to
witness the atrocious spectacle.   The house steward had
his head scalped as by American savages, before death
put a period to his sufferings.   Fourteen persons perished in this manner at Zgorskha, twenty-three at
Zarnow.   At Niedzwiadka, a whole marriage party,
including the bride and bridegroom, were massacred
together in the church where the ceremony was com-
mencing.   In the chateau of M. Bzoski, where a funeral party was assembling, all the parties as they arrived
were slain, and interred in the same grave with the
original deceased."

"THE PEASANTS BORE THE HEADS OF THEIR VICTIMS
ABOUT WITH THEM, AND RECEIVED TEN FLORINS (£1)
FOR EACH, FROM THE LOCAL AUTHORITIES."

"Some of the leaders stained with the worst of these
atrocities, in particular Jaques Szela, were publicly rewarded for their conduct."[*]

Such was the mode in which Austria prepared for
the act by which the free republic of Cracow, although
guaranteed by the treaty of Vienna, was destroyed, and
the city annexed to the Austrian empire.

* Alison's History, vol. vii. p. 581.

of the attacked houses " had been obliged to lead them through the house in search of knives, which they said the prefect of Tarnow told them were concealed in the house, to cut the throats of the peasantry." It is impossible to forget that the Neapolitan crimes were committed under the direction of an Austrian princess, the guilty and ill-fated Caroline of Naples.

This narrative will enable the reader to understand what Henri Martin means by the accusation against the Austrian government of attempting a Gallician policy in Lombardy.

END OF VOL. I.

Billing, Printer and Stereotyper, Guildford, Surrey.

CPSIA information can be obtained
at www.ICGtesting.com
Printed in the USA
BVHW040223050221
599439BV00005B/30

9 781357 716479